THE
CORPORATE
CHRISTIAN
BOOK 2

The Battle For Your Beliefs

PASTOR OWEN E. WILLIAMS

THE CORPORATE CHRISTIAN 2: THE BATTLE FOR
YOUR BELIEFS
Copyright © 2023 by Pastor Owen E. Williams

First edition published 2013.
Second edition published 2023.

Cover Design: 99 Design by Vista
Author Photo: T. L. Holmes
Typesetting: Edge of Water Designs, edgeofwater.com

ISBNs:
   979-8-9874758-6-7 (Paperback)
   979-8-9874758-7-4 (eBook)

Publisher: Grapevine Publishing Press

INTRODUCTION

Belief Systems

Every single living human being on our planet has a belief in something, so what is a belief?

Well, the Oxford American dictionary says it's the thing in which a person has trust and or confidence in. But to go little deeper it's the thing in which you have absolute trust and confidence in; it's what forms our ideologies and philosophies of life and people.

A belief system is a set of mutually supportive beliefs by a group, whether it is religious, philosophical, ideological, social, political, or geographical.

Belief systems are so powerful that they often become the person's or group's identity. In our nation today, a lot of people describe themselves by their belief systems: I am a Christian; I am a Democrat; I am a Republican.

It is said that belief systems are created within social structures when social interaction takes place.

The social interaction is present in the form of doctrine, or rules, which is then learned and understood and stored in the memory system. This memory system consists of two parts, the short-term where the social doctrine is applied through a strategic process through interpretation before it is revealed to the public. The long-term memory is the keeper of all social groups, an attitude. Each of the groups' attitudes represents an array of ideologies which combine to create one's own personal ideology.

The difficulty with Christianity and why it's so hard to make it fit into the social science box is because of a single message that is received by a plural audience from a vast universal array of people, attitudes, and socioeconomic backgrounds.

There is one body, one spirit, just as you were called in one hope of calling, one Lord, one faith, one baptism, one God and Father of all who is above all, and through all and in you all (Ephesians 4:4–6).

So as the *Corporate Christian: Christian Beliefs vs.*

Corporate Behaviors identified the differences of doctrines and behavior that should be displayed by both groups, this book will identify the very *real* tangible attacks and struggles to stay true to your Christian beliefs and the battles, you will have to fight to be successful. Because belief systems are such an intangible part of our human psyche when they are attacked, such attacks can feel very personal. And if the battle is not managed properly it could become very destructive. This is what has happened to the abortion issue; the attacks have become extremely personal to where they are now violent. In our nation today we have very strong national beliefs that, if not managed through the filters of love and peace of the gospel of Christ, can do serious damage to our nation and society—beliefs like gun rights versus gun control and selective immigration enforcement on our southern and northern boarders. So as we begin our journey inward to the motivations of the mind and the satisfactions of soul, always remember that beliefs and belief systems are always a good thing because they provide hope for a better day to come. But, we must never allow the battle for our beliefs to manifest themselves into volatile behavior in the physical world.

"For we wrestle not against flesh and blood but against principalities, against powers, against the rulers of darkness of this world against spiritual wickedness in high places" (Ephesians 6:12). This represents the depth, breath, width, and determination of our enemy. He will never stop coming after us, never stop laying in wait for us, and never stop planning our demise by our own hand through our behavior.

CHAPTER 1

CHRISTIAN BELIEFS

I believe in God, the Father almighty, Creator of heaven and earth and in Jesus Christ, His only son, Our Lord, who was conceived by the Holy Spirit, born of the Virgin Mary, suffered under Pontius Pilate, was crucified, died and was buried, He descended into hell; on the third day He rose again from the dead. He ascended into heaven and is seated at the right hand of God the Father almighty; from there He will come to judge the living and the dead. I believe in the Holy Spirit, the holy Catholic/Universal Church, the communion of the Saints, the forgiveness of sins, the resurrection of the body and life everlasting. Amen (The Apostle's Creed).

The Christian Belief System

As it was previously stated, a belief system is a set of mutually supported beliefs that a group of people have absolute trust and confidence in. In Christianity this belief is not so much in a system but rather in a person—the Lord Jesus Christ. The belief system is completely based on His redeeming, creative, and designing power and His descending, habituating, and ascending works on earth. The three main tenets of this belief system transcend ideology, philosophy, sociology, geography, and politics. It deals with morality, character, and ethics. They are

1. *Salvation:* That if you confess with your mouth the Lord Jesus and believe in your heart that God has raised him from the dead, you will be saved. For with the heart one believes unto righteousness and with the mouth confession is made unto salvation (Romans 10:9–10).

2. *Sanctification:* But sanctify the Lord God in your hearts and always be ready to give a defense to everyone who asks you a reason for the hope that is in you, with meekness and fear (1 Peter 3:15).

3. *Glorification:* Moreover whom He pre- destined, these He also called; whom He called, and these He also justified. And whom He justified, those He also glorified (Romans 8:30).

The Christian believes that salvation is a gift from God and cannot be earned .but it is an honor, duty, and responsibility to live their lives at the highest morale, responsible, and accountable manner. Before I go on let me emphasize that this saving process that the believer believes in, is a very real accountability that one must accept at the end of one's life—how one lives their life and the decisions and *motivations* that we choose and allow to influence us. When being held to the high moral standard of the gospels, any type of rebellious behavior towards this standard is called sin; a sinful person is a rebellious person.

Another part of this belief system is sanctification or holy living. Christ is not only the Lord of our words, but He prefers to be the Lord of our hearts; this is the sanctuary he most prefers to be worshiped in. Once sanctification resides in the heart, holy living follows. This is called the setting-apart period where Christians develop a strong urge to remove themselves from the old behaviors of their life and seek a new way of living, behaving, and talking.

And the last tenet of this belief system is the most important one of this trilogy—glorification. All Christians believe in their hearts that if they keep the faith and belief, fight a good fight to keep their faith and beliefs, and do it to the end of their lives, when their lives are over down here on Earth, they have finished the race well and will hear the precious words of our Lord Jesus "Well done my good and faithful servant, you may enter in." That means they will enter into Heaven and be given glorified bodies, that is a more excellent form of their bodies. For the Christian, glorification is worth all of the struggles and battles they will face in salvation and sanctification.

An example of this process:

Stan is thirty years of age and has a four-year college degree, a good middle management job, and has a salary range of between seventy-five thousand and one-hundred thousand dollars per year. He has recently gotten married and has one child. Stan's family history shows that he was raised in a single-parent household; his mother and father divorced each other when he was ten years old. Stan's mother did the very best she could to provide for him as far as food on the table and a roof over their heads is concerned. But because of the trauma of the divorce and the betrayal of abandonment, Stan's mother became very bitter and angry; her whole view of life became very jaded, and she unconsciously taught this to her son. Stan grew up with a trust-no-one view of life, so he had no one to thank or give credit to. This made Stan a very unsympathetic and cold-hearted man. Now beloved, no man can tell you the day or the hour when you will call on Christ, but the one thing I do know is when you do you will give Him your undivided attention. In Stan's case it was the complete and absolute trust in his own abilities that ignited his pride, which always leads to destruction. Because a proud person can't see past themselves, so they can't see any other solutions or perspectives to life's built-in problems if it does not originate from them. So when Stan lost his job, which was the trophy of his abilities and belief system, he temporarily lost himself. Now what this trauma did to an already angry and jaded person was to open the floodgates to becoming even more so publicly until it started to threaten his marriage, friendships, and mental health. It is only when Stan saw and heard the words that came from his mouth during one of his frequent arguments with his wife that he became ready to acknowledge that something had gone wrong.

Thank God that Stan had some friends who are Christians who invited him to their church where the local pastor was preaching on a topic called "God don't call the qualified but He always qualifies the called." As the pastor started to explain his sermon in detail, he started to talk about the biblical characters in the Book of Hebrews in the eleventh chapter and about how these men's names were mentioned as the Patriarchs of the Faith. The pastor talked about the great accomplishments of these men: how they subdued kingdoms, stopped the mouth of lions, brought down the walls of Jericho, healed the sick, raised the dead, and parted seas. But their personal lives were an utter mess. Some were murderers and fugitives; others were unfaithful to their wives, while others lost their faith. But, as the pastor explained, what made them men of great faith was not what they brought to the call but what they were willing to trust God with in their lives. They understood that their call was perfect and that they were not and needed to be developed by God to walk in the call He had for them.

This message stayed with Stan, and in the midst of his situation, he pondered about these biblical men, their circumstances, and his own. It brought Stan to the realization that you don't have to be the best at anything in life or be perfect all the time just to avoid having to ask or depend on somebody or anybody. If you trust in God and allow Him to lead and guide you, there will be more inner peace in your life. This process and outcome is based on the symbiotic relationship between faith and belief.

Faith and Belief

Now faith is the substance of thing hoped for, the evidence of things not seen. For by it the elders obtained a good report (Hebrews 11:1–2).

This relationship between faith and belief is demonstrated everyday in how we as believers in Christ, as well as nonbelievers, respond to life's built-in problems. Faith by itself is a theological word that operates in the spiritual realm: now faith is the substance of things hoped for. It's saying that in the spirit realm your faith is really substantive and solid. It's your confidence in the unseen, God.

But faithfulness is an ethical word that operates in the natural realm. Most men will proclaim each his own goodness, but who can find a faithful man? (Proverbs 20:6)

Faithful behavior is ethical, trustworthy, dependable, and accountable behavior, driven by the Christian's belief in Christ. It is anchored in the last three fruit of the spirit which deal with personal development: *faithfulness, meekness,* and *self control.* These three behaviors deal with the maturation and development of a believer. Are you an ethical and trustworthy person; can you keep your word? Are you a powerful person yet focused and humble, not always seeking to be the center of attention? Are you a person who exercises self control and can control your appetites and emotions?

When this process is active, it ushers peace into the person's life, and peace is such a precious commodity in today's society that most people value it more than money. Jesus Himself said this to us: "Peace I leave with you, my peace I give unto you, not as the world giveth, give I unto you. Let not your heart be troubled, neither let it be afraid" (John 14:27).

There are many things in life that money can't begin to protect us from, but peace brings calm in the midst of all stress. Philippians 4:7 says "and the peace of God, which passeth all understanding, shall keep your hearts and minds through Christ Jesus."

There is something about being at peace within yourself, your family, and your job. It ushers in and sustains joy and happiness—something money rarely does. This kind of peace is addictive and contagious. When one tastes it, they never want to live without it in their lives.

In this environment beliefs become stronger and clearer, and a better understanding of one's faith is revealed.

There is a reason why Christ asked his disciples to pray for the peace of Jerusalem: "they shall prosper that love thee."(Psalms 122:6) Only through peace come prosperity, security, *beauty*, tranquility, and harmony. These are things money and power could never achieve. No wonder Stan became so engulfed in this new way of living and perceiving of life. In this environment beliefs become stronger and clearer with a better understanding of your faith being revealed.

Belief in whom:

> That if thou shalt confess with thy mouth the Lord Jesus and shalt believe in thine heart that God hath raised him from the dead, thou shalt be saved for with the heart man believeth unto righteousness and with the mouth confession is made unto salvation (Romans 10:9-10).

As we stated earlier the Christian belief system is all about who and not what, but we tend to misinterpret our relationship to Him. So let us take a quick theological trip to how we ended up with this belief system that is based on our relationship with Christ. Biblical theology tells us that from the beginning of humanity God has been striving and driving us towards this relationship. The entire Bible is based on eight foundational covenants between God and mankind. And they are in the following order:

- *The Edenic Covenant:* this is a conditional covenant found in Genesis 1:26–31; 2:16–17. It outlines man's responsibility towards creation and God's directive regarding the tree of knowledge of good and evil. God's conditional promise to Adam was that blessings and curses depend on the faithfulness of mankind.

- *The Adamic Covenant:* this is an unconditional covenant found in Genesis 3:16–19. God pronounce to Adam what kind of hard- ships he can expect in life because of his sin. In this meeting between God and Adam, Adam represents all of humanity to come. He is called the first Adam.

- *The Noahic Covenant:* this is also an unconditional covenant, found in Genesis 9:1–18. God made a promise to Noah and his sons after the flood waters receded and everyone left the ark. God caused a rainbow to appear in the sky on that day and used it to promise Noah as well as all mankind, that He would never again destroy the Earth and all its inhabitants in a worldwide flood.

- *The Abrahamic Covenant:* this is an unconditional covenant found in Genesis 12:1–4; 13:14–17; 15:1–7; 17:1–8. God made a promise to Abraham that he would be the father of many different nations of people and that he would prosper and be blessed. The Jewish race came through the seed of Abraham, and the sign of the covenant is circumcision.

- *The Mosaic Covenant:* this is a conditional covenant that God made between himself and Moses and is found in Exodus 20:1–31; 18. In this covenant God gave the Ten Commandments to the Hebrew people so they could know His will and know how to govern the people. It's a developmental covenant.

- *The Land Covenant or "Palestine Covenant":* this unconditional covenant is the promise God made to the Israelites about the land He would give to them for their own. The covenant also includes the provision that when the land was given, the Israel people would be united again. This is found Deuteronomy 30:1–10.

- *The Davidic Covenant:* this is an unconditional covenant from God to David that he would have an eternal dynasty. This is found in 2 Samuel 7:4–16 and 1 Chronicles 17:3–15. God's promise to David is based on three main principles: The first one is an everlasting throne, the second is an everlasting king, and the third is an everlasting kingdom (Daniel 7:14).

- *The New Covenant:* this covenant is mentioned many times throughout the Old Testament to promise a future messianic age. This is an unconditional covenant that was established between God and all of humanity—whoever chooses to accept a life of obedience—to a new source of eternal salvation. "And having been perfected, He became the author of eternal salvation to all who obeyed him" (Hebrews 5:9).

So you see, beloved, our Christian belief is based on Jesus Christ and God's promises of a future messianic age. In this new promise, Christ is the Deliverer and Savior of all who confess and believe in Him. We are free to choose him and be free from the conditional law of the Mosaic covenant. In this new covenant, Christ represents a more perfect second Adam who stands for all of mankind that belongs to him, where the first Adam stood, failed, and fell. Christ stands and will never fail or fall, guaranteeing our eternal glorification. This is the living definition of Hebrews 11:1 that says, "Now faith is the substance of things hoped for the evidence of things not yet seen." Our confidence in the unseen future is real and very *substantive*.

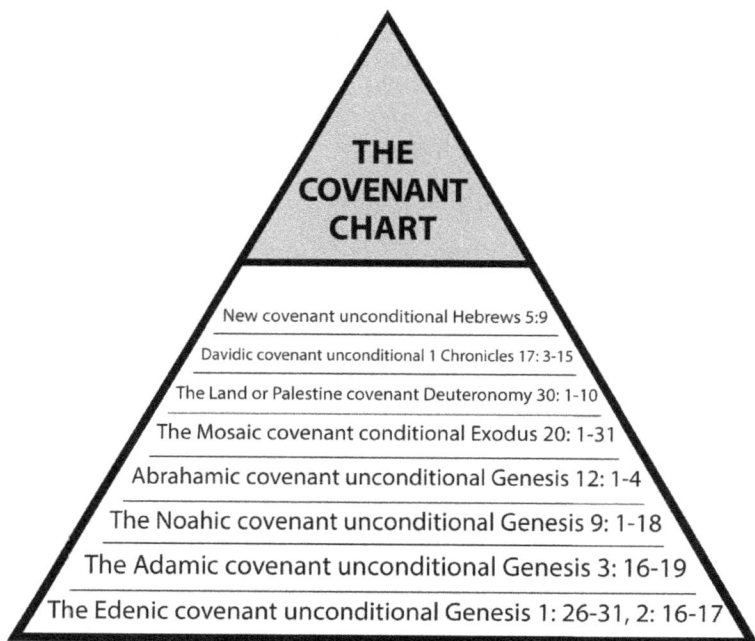

THE COVENANT CHART

New covenant unconditional Hebrews 5:9

Davidic covenant unconditional 1 Chronicles 17: 3-15

The Land or Palestine covenant Deuteronomy 30: 1-10

The Mosaic covenant conditional Exodus 20: 1-31

Abrahamic covenant unconditional Genesis 12: 1-4

The Noahic covenant unconditional Genesis 9: 1-18

The Adamic covenant unconditional Genesis 3: 16-19

The Edenic covenant unconditional Genesis 1: 26-31, 2: 16-17

Motivation for Belief

> But they have not all obeyed the gospel, for
> Isaiah says, "Lord who has believed our report?"
> So then faith comes by hearing and hearing the
> word of God. But I say, "Have they not heard?
> Yes indeed: Their sound has gone out to all the
> Earth and their words to the end of the world
> (Romans 10:16–18).

The Bible says faith comes by hearing the word, but in Israel's case this was not what happened. As a matter of fact, they heard it and rejected it.

The verses just prior to Romans 10:16–18 say, "How then shall they call on Him in whom they have not believed? And how shall they believe in Him of whom they have not heard? And how shall they preach unless they are sent? As it is written, 'How beautiful are the feet of those who preach the gospel of peace, who bring glad tidings of good things'" (Romans 10:14–15).

Even so, they still disobeyed the good news. So the question is, what motivates a person to start to believe in and follow Christ? In my limited experience, very rarely do people hear the word and then receive the word. Because this is always a life- changing decision in someone's life, it always takes a life-changing event to bring it to fruition.

Jim Rohn, in his book *The Treasury of Quotes*, says these two things:

"Disgust and resolve are two great emotions that lead to change," and "We generally change ourselves for one or two reasons: Inspiration or Desperation."

These quotes are accurate as they seem to point us to the opinion that life-changing events lead and drive us into life-changing decisions. The dilemma with this quagmire is, what is the right decision?

An example of this is when you are going through a stormy period in your life. The one constant is to keep going through, but in these stressful periods there is a tendency to stop, turn around, and look for some avenue of escape. If you are experiencing difficulties on your job due to performance or relationship problems, looking for another job may not always be the first best option, even though it may be the most appealing one. I believe this response comes from our stubborn reluctance to change. Changing one's environment is one thing but changing your thinking and behavior is a very difficult thing to do.

Jim Rohn also quoted this, "I find it fascinating that most people plan their vacation with better care than they do their lives. Perhaps that is because escape is easier than change."

Well Mr. Rohn, I agree with your quote because the Bible supports it:

I call Heaven and Earth as witnesses today against you, that I have set before you life and death, blessing and cursing; therefore choose life, that both you and your descendants may live. Deuteronomy 30:19.

I am the door. If anyone enters by me, he will be saved and will go in and out and find pasture. The thief does not come except to steal, and to kill and to destroy. I have come that they may have life, and they may have it more abundantly (John 10:9-10).

Life is a never ending journey of choices; the Bible is a book about decisions to complete the journey of life well, so choose life and the abundance of it.

So after a life-changing event blows into your life and disrupts the normalcy of it, what was once certain now becomes uncertain, decisions that once were clear are now cloudy, and attitudes that were once positive now become negative. Right here is where the battle will be set; here is where how long and how hard the fight is will be determined.

The campaign against us is to get us to believe in (and act upon) what the believer in Christ calls the fruit of the flesh, rather than the fruit of the Spirit. This will be discussed in more detail as we get fur- ther along into the book.

CHAPTER 2

CORPORATE BEHAVIORS:
THE MORALITY OF MANAGEMENT

For unto us a child is born, unto us a son
is given; and the government will be upon His
shoulder and His name will be called Wonderful,
Counselor, Mighty God, Everlasting Father, Prince
of Peace. Of the increase of His government of
peace there will be no end, upon the throne of
David and over His kingdom, to order it and
establish it with judgment and justice from
that time forward, even forever. The zeal of the
Lord of hosts will perform this (Isaiah 9:6–7).

When we speak about corporate behaviors we are really talking about leadership qualities and behavior. When the prophet Isaiah penned the above scripture, it was meant to be an example for all who govern and lead to follow.

Before we go into the example I must first explain the meaning of the scripture passage, which will then make the example more understandable.

Beloved, know that to understand this scripture, one must link it next to Romans 13:1: "Let every soul be subject to governing authorities. For there is no authority except from God and the authorities that exist are appointed by God."

As we look at the scripture passage from Isaiah, we see that it describes a personal relationship between the governing and the governed. It says for unto us a child is born unto us a son is given, from among us a child is born and to us a son has been given. In other words He comes from us and He belongs to us and we to Him, and only because of this close personal relationship from Him to us are these descriptive adjectives used to describe how He will govern us.

Wonderful Counselor: Divine supernatural wisdom will be the norm in how He discharges delegates and determines His office and responsibilities. He is not just a Counselor but a Wonderful Counselor, not just God but Mighty God, not just Father but Everlasting Father. The adjectives describe the quality of His leadership.

Mighty God: He is the symbol of a powerful protective warrior who will and can succeed against any type of natural challenges.

Everlasting Father: A Father to His people always displaying care, compassion, concern, and intimacy to all who belong to Him.

This is the standard for all governments in authority to follow, but until this standard becomes the normal reality, we all must be subjected to Romans 13:1, in which God is asking all of us for absolute obedience to civil authority with one exception, which is when civil authority is in disobedience to God's word and puts itself above God's word and law.

> Shadrach, Meshach and Abednego answered and said to the king "O" Nebuchadnezzar we have no need to answer you in this matter. If that is the case, our God whom we serve is able to deliver us from the burning fiery furnace, and He will deliver us from your hand, O King. But if not, let it be known to you, O King that we do not serve your gods, nor will we worship the gold image which you have set up (Daniel 3:16–18).

Now it's important to understand that you have rights as a believer in Christ to resist authority when authority violates the word of God. This does not include issues of our own pride and ego, not because some states have legalized abortion, not because some states have legalized gay marriage—none of these politically charged issues that reflect the limitations of carnal wisdom. But when authority places itself above

God and demands that its citizens worship or pray to it, when human authority subverts Gods authority on equality and reclassifies the worth of human being, this is the time for civil dissent. It is the time for civil dissent, when authority engages in mass murder and genocide and when human authority causes discord among the brethren. In the absence of these things, we all must be obedient to the human authority that is placed over us. God in His divine wisdom has established four levels of governments on the earth:

- Secular governments for all citizens
- The Church for all believers
- Parents for all children
- Employers for all employees

To be most effective in their purpose, all of these authorities require obedience.

Overt Behaviors

Overt Behaviors are defined as open and unconcealed public actions.

And when you pray, do not be like the hypocrites, for they love to pray standing in the synagogues and on the street corners to be seen by men. I tell you the truth; they have received their rewards in full (Matthew 6:5).

The Pharisee stood up and prayed about himself, "God, I thank you that I am not like other men, robbers, evildoers, adulterers or even like this tax collector." (Luke 18:11).

Beloved, in my almost-thirty years of working in the corporate environment, it's a very rare thing to see a completely selfless act when it comes to moving and maneuvering oneself through the corporate environment. As a matter of fact, it's a mandate for those who are not walking according to the spirit but rather after the flesh, to adopt selfish ambitions as a way of corporate life due to the competitive nature of the work environment. Television shows like *The Apprentice* and *Survivor* crystallize this mindset.

The trick here is to recognize the overt behavior in its setting or market, and then catalog it as moral behavior or immoral behavior. The generic definition of morality is the differentiation of intentions, decisions, and actions between those that are good and right and those that are bad and wrong. The philosophy of morality is ethics; it is ethical behavior on display.

Ethical people are faithful and trustworthy people; they are first and foremost faithful to their beliefs and trusted not to violate them no matter how great the temptation is to do so. This is where the battle for your beliefs begins.

Covert Behaviors

When we talk about covert behaviors, we are talking about concealed, secret, or disguised behavior, behaviors that show one thing but have completely different intentions.

Most people participate in covert behavior because

in their hearts they know their intentions are wrong or bad. For example, most forms of adultery are always done covertly because if done publicly they would attract the wrong attention and opinions from others about the participant's moral code, choices, and conduct.

When They Are Applied:

Beloved, a very big part of being victorious in anything is timing: what play to call and execute at what time. Knowing when is the right time is all about discernment, that discriminating awareness and acuteness of judgment and understanding of what is actually being said and displayed in front of and around you.

In the scripture Matthew 6:5, Christ asks us not to be hypocrites, performers, or actors of life but rather be livers of life and live it more abundantly. Because there is a war going on all around us in the unseen spiritual realm, and the prize are your beliefs, then your behaviors, and ultimately your soul.

In the fifth chapter of the Epistle to the Galatians, the apostle Paul lays out in graphic detail this conflict from the eleventh verse. He says this: "I say then:

Walk in the spirit and you shall not fulfill the lust of the flesh, for the flesh lusts against the spirit and the spirit against the flesh; and these are contrary to one another. So that you do not do the things that you wish. But if you are led by the spirit, you are not under the law.

As stated earlier, this war is for your manifested behavior, which can alter or disqualify your belief in Christ in your own mind. Allow me to lay out exactly what is happening in this campaign against you, the believer. The fifth chapter of the Epistle to the Galatians says this: When you, the believer in Christ, come to Him for the first time, He receives you and you receive Him as your Lord and Savior, He takes you in with all of your flawed humanity as you also take Him in with all of His perfect divinity. In this process you are giving your life to Him and allowing Him, or deferring to Him, to regulate how we think, perceive, and behave. You are accepting a new nature, His nature. This beloved is called the born-again doctrine that Christ spoke to Nicodemus the Pharisee.

Jesus answered and said to him, "Most assuredly, I say to you unless one is born again, he cannot see the kingdom of God." Nicodemus said to Him, "How can a man be born when he is old? Can he enter a second time into his mother's womb and be born?" Jesus answered, "Most assuredly, I say to you unless one is born of water and the spirit, he cannot enter the kingdom of God. That which is born of flesh is flesh, and that which is born of the spirit is spirit. Do not marvel that I said to you, you must be born again. The wind blows where it wishes and you hear the sound of it but cannot tell where it comes from and where it goes. So is everyone who is born of the spirit" (John 3:3–8).

So being born of water and the spirit is the spiritual cleansing and purification of one's soul, which is the center seat of man from where thoughts, perceptions, feeling and behavior originate. As the wind cannot be controlled or understood by humans, but the effects of the wind can be witnessed, is like the Holy Spirit, who cannot be controlled or understood, but his effect on peoples, thoughts, perceptions, behaviors, and lives are very apparent.

In this process, the Holy Spirit resides in us and is in constant conflict with our old nature. The new nature is called the Spirit nature; whereas the old nature is called the flesh—but understand that I'm not referring to skin and bones. Here our flesh nature is everything we were before believing in Christ. It is our old ways, old perceptions, old thoughts, motivations, and desires.

This old nature is so powerful and hardwired into

us that the only way to get free from it is to reboot the whole system but even with this, the old nature is still very much alive and present in our daily lives. So while the system is rebooting, a new nature is introduced into the system and the wonderful and saving power of this new nature is that it comes fully compatible and complete in all things of power, knowledge, wisdom, relations, and life. All we have to do is learn it and trust it.

The Conflict:

We need to be very clear on this, there is no scenario where our flesh nature could ever be involved in a successful conflict against Christ's nature, yet still we are in a conflict, So where is the battle and how is it being fought? To understand this let us first identify what is human nature.

Most sociologists and philosophers would agree that human nature is distinguishing characteristics of how we think, feel, and act. This tends to be done independent of culture. What has never been concretely established is what causes it or if it is *fixed* and woven into our physical development as a species.

The answers to these questions would have important implications on ethics, politics, and even theology. This is because human nature can be regarded as both a source of norms of conduct and a way of life. This is very important because it's going to address a very old question, and that is, are people born bad or do they learn bad behavior? Well, as a man of faith and a believer in the teachings of Christ, I believe that all behavior is learned, but I also believe that there are evil influences all around us that tempt and prod us into evil acts.

Passion and Propensity

In the realm of beliefs, surviving the attacks and getting the victory all depend on your passion and your propensity. Isaiah 9:6–7, quoted at the beginning of this chapter, ended with this verse: "The zeal of the Lord of host will perform this." Beloved for Christ to be our Wonderful Counselor, Mighty God, Everlasting Father, and Prince of Peace He first had to have a zeal, eager desire, and enthusiastic diligence to perform it. He had to have passion; Christ was so passionate about this that He came down from glory so divinity could live among humanity, incorruption among corruption. He put Himself in the hands of vicious and ignorant men who victimized and brutalized Him all the way to Calvary. So in Christ's case His passion for His call strengthened His propensity to endure all of the trials and tribulations of the Christian life.

You see your victory in this battle will depend on how much passion you have for your belief and how much you can endure to get the victory.

An example of this is: A young woman by the name of Ann gave her life to Christ at the age of thirty-five. She has two teenage boys and worked in the male-dominated sales industry. Prior to her conversion she found it very hard to deal with and function in the environment of sexually inappropriate language, gender bias policies, and the never-ending stress to meet the sales numbers the industry demands. It led her to indulge in nightly glasses of wine to help her sleep, a more abrupt and angry tone to her conversations, and a very cold demeanor. She was very unhappy with the direction her life was going in but felt she could not change it because she could not leave her job; she had two children to support. The never-ending rock and a hard place were in effect. When Ann came to Christ, she was at her wits end emotionally and psychologically. She was looking for peace—any kind would do. The nightcaps were not working anymore and were leading to addictive behaviors, but she found that in Christ, there is not addiction just restoration. Ann began to develop a relationship with Christ and *learned* that in Christ all things are new and old things pass away. She understood to be her new nature, her new outlook on the same old life, her new perspective to the same old issues, and her new speech, tone, and attitude, and she felt tremendous peace within. She realized that her old outlook upon her life was *attracting* and magnifying negativity, chaos, and confusion. Her old nature could not let go of the past and how she was treated, and she had personalized all the issues, which kept her in a very depressed state. While simultaneously hoping for a breakthrough of a better job or a winning lottery ticket, this futuristic mindset kept her in a state of anxiousness as well. So you see Ann had a lot of motivation to seek Christ and be delivered from her circumstances. As she developed and grew in gospel maturity, her whole outlook on her circumstances changed; she no longer saw herself as a victim, living in a pity party state of existence, but rather saw her tormentors as the victims to their own impulses and urges. Once this trauma was removed from her emotional life, she developed an attitude of gratitude for the simplest things that God gave to her on a daily basis: her children, all of the family's life, health, and daily strength, a job to supply the needs of her family, her new relationship with Christ, the Church, and the saints, and a wonderful opportunity to witness to her tormentors. Her born- again experience, unbeknownst to her, gave her a new belief system that came with a very gratifying emotional, spiritual, and psychological benefit.

CHAPTER 3

ATTACKS

And from the days of John the Baptist until now the Kingdom of heaven suffers violence's and the violent take it by force (Matthew 11:12).

The law and the prophets were until John. Since that time the kingdom of God has been preached, and everyone is pressing into it (Luke 16:16).

Even since John the Baptist started preaching the gospel of Jesus Christ, it has always evoked a strong response from the world, and the response is always to silence the message by either disqualifying or *destroying* the messenger as was the fate of the Baptist and Christ. As believers, however, we are not to run from this violence, but rather we are to press directly into it.

Beloved, the Apostle Paul made this battle the centerpiece of his entire life, and he summed up his life this way.

> Brethren, I do not count myself to have apprehended, but one thing I do, forgetting those things which are behind and reaching forward to those things which are ahead, I press toward the goal for the prize of the upward call of God in Christ Jesus (Philippians 3:13–14).

Beloved, Paul was very honest with himself as to what kind of man he was and what kind of man he wanted to be, so he says he really has not attained his goal as of yet, but the main and only thing in his life that he deemed important was to forget any past virtuous deeds or *accolades* that have been achieved in ministry and life. They only give one a false reality of one's self, so forget them, don't rest on them, and always keep reaching and pressing forward for Christ likeness, which is the true and only goal of the upward call in God.

For the attack is designed to distort and distract you from attaining Christ likeness and cause you to pursue unrighteousness in word and deeds.

The Realm of the Attack

"For we do not wrestle against flesh and blood, but against principalities, against powers, against the rulers of the darkness of this age, against spiritual host of wickedness in the heavenly places"

This attack against you will be launched from the spiritual realm, so your weapons cannot come from the carnal realm to defend yourself, because even though this attack originates in the spiritual realm the effects and consequences will be seen and felt in the physical one.

But please don't misunderstand me, it is not my intention to make you seem powerless from these attacks, even though you will never have the power to stop the attack, you do have the power to successfully defend yourself every time one is launched at you. And the best defense is always based on sound information.

Three Kinds of Attacks

Dr. David Jeremiah, the Senior Pastor of the Shadow Mountain Community Church in San Diego, California, says the enemy (Satan) has only three ways to attack us, and they are *the expected attack, the unexpected attack,* and *the unfounded attack*.

> ➤ **The Expected Attack:**
> If Satan, our sworn enemy, is best described as a roaring lion, we should always expect to be attacked when in the presence of a lion.

The lion represents the threat of expected attacks against our lives and families. This is life. It always comes with built-in problems, and no life will be problem-free.

There will be relationship problems between husbands and wives, fathers and sons, mothers and daughters, and employers and employees. There will be financial problems, too much debt, not enough income, and loss of homes and cars. There will be health problems: sickness in the body, depression in the spirit, or anger in the attitude. There will also be problems in the ministry that include disobedience, mistrust, gossip, envy, jealousy, and pride.

Because of these built-in life problems, we should always accept God's promise of divine protection for us. He promised that whomever "dwells in the secret place of the Most High shall abide under the shadow of the Almighty. I will say of the Lord, *"He is* my refuge and my fortress; My God, in Him I will trust" (Psalm 91:1–2). Because of the ever-present dangers and terrors that surround humanity, God provides ongoing, sovereign protection for his people.

> ➤ **The Unexpected Attack:**

Moses said if we stay under the protection of the Almighty we will be delivered from the snares of the fowler.

These snares are the plots against us that intend to endanger our lives. Serpents, like the adder or moccasin, lay in wait undercover of anything like a rock, a leaf, or a bush, and when they attack you rarely see it coming. The accident, the job loss, that problem—it was just lying there under the rock, and you didn't see it coming.

The unexpected attack can be very frightening because of the element of surprise. It catches us off guard. We feel overwhelming fear in the moment. When we find ourselves in that moment, we should not freak out but rather calmly run into the shadow of the Almighty and know that miracles can strike just as suddenly as tragedies.

Beloved we can learn a lot from the Apostle Paul's example when he was struck suddenly by a viper that was lying in wait.

In the book Acts, the twenty-eighth chapter, we see the story of Paul's ministry on Malta and how he survived the snakebite. As the scriptures describe, while on their way to Rome the ship encountered a severe storm and was shipwrecked on the Greek island of Malta. After surviving the stormy waters and making it to shore, the survivors including the Apostle Paul were greeted by some very sympathetic and gracious natives.

The scripture describes that while they were gathering wood to light a fire for warmth, a viper was hiding under one of the logs, and as Paul reached for the log it fastened itself to his hand. He calmly shook it off into the flames of the newly lit fire and went on about his business.

When a snake attacks you unexpectedly don't let it hang on to you and continue to chew on your mind, emotions, thoughts, and your family. Shake it off. During this stage of the unexpected attack, your peace, joy, relation- ships, faith, and trust are in jeopardy through the sneaky accusations that come to your mind. Satan is a joy killer and hope stealer. He truly comes to kill, steal, and destroy all of you, but El Shaddai will cleanse our hearts from the chewing adder. He will destroy the trauma of the unexpected attack on your life. He will restore to you all what the enemy will try to steal.

Beloved, I've seen how this kind of attack works up close and personal. I am a witness to it firsthand. About twenty.years ago, with great joy I expected to move into my new home with my young family and embark on a life filled with joy evermore.

But then that snake took my job, and I did not see it coming. Then he took my business, and I did not see that coming, either. These events put me in a state of depression, which gave him an advantage point to try to take my marriage, my joy, my peace, my faith, and, yes, even my life. But beloved, I know for myself that he who dwells in the secret place of the Most High will abide in the shadow of the Almighty for in His presence is the fullness of joy and pleasures evermore.

➢ **The Unfounded Attack:**

Smoke and mirrors are the foundation of Satan's unfounded attack. He tries to intimidate us and keep us from going beyond a certain point in our walk with God in our lives. This is done through fear of the unknown. The enemy says, "Don't dream beyond this point; don't reach for anything more. Don't do this, don't do that . . .we never did that here before. Black people don't live in these kinds of neighborhoods; women can't do these kinds of jobs, and on and on.

Beloved, through intimidation the dragon devours us by stopping us from pursuing our dreams. But with God there are no boundaries, only possibilities. God said "As it is written, I have made thee a father of many nations before God, whom he believed, who quickened the dead, and *called those things that are not as those they are*" (Romans, 4:17).

I have also experienced this kind of attack first hand. About thirty-four years ago, I was a junior in high school in Miami, Florida, when a life-changing opportunity was presented to my mother. A local U.S. Congressman offered my mother an opportunity for me to go to the Air Force Academy in Colorado Springs, Colorado. It came through an Air Force Colonel who was a friend of the family. As this opportunity was presented to me, I was in the tenth or eleventh grade of high school and should have known how great a blessing this was, but the only things I saw was my own psychological limitation. The first thing that came to my mind was race; I would be the only black person there, and I did not want to be in that situation. The second thing was education, I was terrible in mathematics and thought I could never make it through four years in that place. I systematically allowed my inferiority complex and low self-esteem issues, along with the fear of the unknown, to talk me out of what would be worth in today's dollars a couple-hundred-thou- sand-dollar education, yes, I was a victim of the unfounded attack. But with the right battle plan, you never have to be a victim of these attacks.

The Design of the Attack

The three attacks (expected, unexpected, and unfounded) are designed to work in conjunction with the three windows in which sin enters into our heart:

- The lust of the flesh
- The pride of life
- The lust of the eyes

When Christ started His earthly ministry He went into the wilderness to fast for forty days and forty nights, and Satan tempted and attacked Him three times.

The first attack was designed to stimulate the body's desire for food, so he came at Him this way: because you are the son of God, command that these stones to become bread. This was designed to get Him, because of His hunger, to violate the plan of God for His life and employ the divine power that He had set aside.

When you purpose in your heart to start to make a change, you can expect the attack (an expected attack) in the form of someone who comes and tries to talk and tempt you back to the old ways and cause you to violate your purpose and resolution.

The second attack was designed to stimulate the

pride that all human beings feel: it's that side of pride that manifests arrogance and condescending attitudes in us because we feel better or more special than someone else due to a certain accomplishment or achievement. Even though each and every one of us is unique and special in the sight of God, with our very own gifts and places designed for where our gifts will flourish, it's not our place to test God with prideful and reckless behaviors, no matter how much confidence we have about ourselves.

In Jesus' temptation, Satan twisted the scriptures from Psalm 91:11, 12: "For He shall give His angels charge over you, to keep you in all your ways. In their hands they shall bear you up, lest you dash your foot against a stone." As he quoted this scripture back to Jesus, he twisted its meaning from trusting God to doubting Him, therefore testing Him to see if He would do as His word says He would. Prideful people don't like to be dependent on anybody or anything; they must always be in charge and control. Pride always goes before a fall, because prideful folks never see the unexpected attack.

The third attack was designed in the form of an exploitive bribe. As the god of this age, Satan controls the kingdoms of the earth and can give them to whom he pleases on the condition of complete allegiance to him.

So beloved when the *expected attack* comes, so will the temptation of relief from the problem—if you are willing to violate something you swore before God. When the *unexpected attack* comes, so will the temptation of prideful, reckless, ungodly behavior to put doubt between you and God, and finally when the *unfounded attack* comes, so will the temptation of exploitation telling you that you can have all you desire and be all you can be if you violate what God has designed for you.

Beloved, as you can see this attack is complex, and Satan has been doing it since the Garden of Eden. The Hebrew children went into the wilderness and a generation died there because they kept being defeated by these attacks—because they were fighting a spiritual war with carnal weapons. Jesus went into the wilderness and got the victory every time because He used spiritual weapons—the word of God.

> For the weapons of our warfare are not carnal but mighty in God for the pulling down of strong holds, casting down arguments and every high thing that exalts itself against the knowledge of God, bringing every thought into captivity to the obedience of Christ (2 Corinthians 10:3-5).

This is the word of God, the sword of the Spirit, which is our only needed offense weapon against Satan.

So, beloved, when you are under attack, don't run, don't hide; just follow the Apostle Paul's advice in Ephesians 6:10:

> Finally, my brother be strong in the Lord and in the power of His might and stand therefore, having girded your waste with truth, having put

on the breast plate of righteousness and having shod your feet with the preparation of the gospel of peace and press directly into the violence taking hold of Christ likeness.

CHAPTER 4

THE RESPONSE

But sanctify the Lord God in your hearts and always be ready to give a defense to everyone who asks you a reason for the hope that is in you, with meekness and fear; having a good conscience, that when they defame you as evildoers, those who revile your good conduct in Christ may be ashamed. For it is better, if it is the will of God, to suffer for doing well than for doing evil (1 Peter 3:15–17).

Preparing for a Response

B eloved, all attacks that come upon us produce an environment of trauma, and most of it is in the form of emotional and psychological trauma, which deeply affects the mind and our decision-making abilities. If the response is not the right one, it could escalate the violence of the attacks or transform you from the victim to an angry, vengeful attacker.

In the last chapter, we talked about the attacks and the differences between them, and based on this knowledge, this is how one should always prepare to respond after being attacked.

The scripture at the beginning of this chapter said to sanctify the Lord in your heart. Beloved, this is the place the Lord most prefers to be worshiped, not just in our praise, our songs, or our works, but mostly in our hearts. Why? Because the heart is the place where the Lord can motivate and orchestrate behavior.

In my first book, *The Corporate Christian: Christian*

Beliefs vs. Corporate Behaviors, I talked about a doctrine call the fruit of the spirit, but I dealt with this doctrine from a theological point of view. In this chapter, I would like to come from a more psychological development perspective.

The Public Response

When I talk about a public response, what I am talking about is the observed, physical, emotional, and psychological behavior that is on display during, through, and after a traumatic attack takes place. Only through cognitive development of the scriptures and spiritual development in a relationship with Christ can one manage the response properly and righteously.

In Galatians 5:22, 23, it says this: "but the fruit of the spirit is love, joy, peace, longsuffering, kindness, goodness, faithfulness, gentleness, self-control. Against such there is not law." Beloved, as born-again believers in Christ, it is not enough to stop doing the bad and wrong things we used to always do, but rather we should strive to mature to Christ likeness by letting the Holy

Spirit manifest the life, mind, and attitudes of Christ in us; which is the fruit of the Holy Spirit.

As you look at the fruit of the Holy Spirit you will notice that there are nine of them, and they are divided into three categories of three. They are targeted to our personality for our development. This development process is divided into three primary foundations of our lives.

➢ Our Personal Development in Our Experience with God
  • Love
  • Joy
  • Peace

➢ Our Personal Development in our relationship with Others
  • Longsuffering
  • Kindness
  • Goodness

➤ Our Personal Development as People
- Faithfulness
- Meekness
- Self-control

As we grow in Christ and develop and mature in our attitudes and character, we begin to allow these fruit to transform our nature so it can no longer be provoked by the fiery darts of the world. Let's look at how these fruit work.

The First Three: Developing Our Personal Experience with God.

When humanity comes into the presence of divinity, the experience is always drastically life changing and this result is always based on what primary overpowering forces our nature encounters during this meeting.

The foundational attributes in the character of God are *love, joy,* and *peace.* Because love is the primary evidence of the presence of the Spirit of God in a person's life, it must also be the foundational fruit in our character. "And we have known and believed the love that God has for us. God is love, and he who abides in love abides in God and God in him" (1 John 4:16). It is also the primary command of God "You shall love the Lord your God with all your heart and with all your soul and with all you might" (Deuteronomy 6:5).

Love is the foundation of our faith: "for God so loved the world that He gave His only begotten so, that whoever believes in Him shall not perish but have everlasting life" (John 3:16).

Now joy also is the evidence of the Holy Spirit in a person's life; this is because Jesus is the center of our joy. "These things I have spoken to you, that my joy may remain in you and that your joy may be full" (John 15:11).

This type of joy is deeply seated in the soul of the believer. Storms may blow in and out of our lives; attacks may come and go, and while this joy may seem to disappear for a while, in the morning Joy will arise with the dawn of the new day. "For the joy of the Lord is our strength" (Nehemiah 8:10).

In other words, Holy Spirit joy keeps our sorrow from turning into despair and depression. Life may produce difficult circumstances and situations, but there is absolute certainty that the Holy Spirit joy in our lives will survive it all.

Peace, like joy, is also evidence of the Holy Spirit in a person life, and like joy, Jesus is the center of our peace. The beauty of our peace is that it is not produced by anything of this world. It does not come from a fishing trip, solitude, or a Caribbean vacation. Beloved, everlasting peace is given to us by Jesus Christ. "Peace I leave with you, my peace I give to you and not as the world gives do I give to you. Let not your heart be troubled, neither let it be afraid" (John 14:27).

It is absolute and complete in spite of circum- stances that happen in life, whether it be on a national or local level from super storm Sandy to the massacre at Sandy Hook. Christ says, "These things I have spoken to you, that in Me you may have peace. In the world you will have tribulations, but be of good cheer, I have overcome the world" (John 16:33).

Love, Joy, and Peace are three emotions the human spirit craves for its entire life on earth; so when it is found missing, developing it becomes an integral part of our life and character as a desired necessity.

The Second Three: Developing Our Personal Relationship with Our Friends and Coworkers

These fruit are designed to develop us in our personal relationships with other people. We have been designed to be social beings, spreading a social message called the Gospel or Good News. Even though the message is perfect and the messenger is not, how it is spread is always crucial to its success. In developing our relationships, God has asked us to make three personality traits primary in our character for dealing and interacting in personal, work, family, business, and social relationships.

Patience: We should always have patience or be long-tempered, never short-tempered in our relationships with others. An individual with a long temper or patience stays in control of his or her feelings when dealing with other people.

As we all know, relationships can be very trying and tempers often get short, but the temper which is produced by the Holy Spirit is long, patient, and in control under pressure; it is longsuffering.

Kindness is another vital personality trait that the Holy Spirit manifests in our lives. As we all too often see and know in our society, culture, and world today, people show and demonstrate far too little kindness. It seems to be a lost art, and this produces a downward spiral of unkind and disrespectful behavior on our jobs, in traffic, and on the bus or train. Folks don't act kind so people don't expect kindness, and when people don't expect it there is less motivation to be kind to anyone—and down the spiral goes.

But the kindness imparted unto our soul from the

Holy Spirit is not motivated by our expectation of what others do or don't do. It is based on the presence of the Holy Spirit in our lives. "And be kind to one another, tender hearted forgiving one another even as God in Christ forgave you" (Ephesians 4:32).

Goodness comes about because of the first two fruit in this second group. It is when people describe your relationship with them as a good one because you are patient and kind. You will often hear someone say this about a person: "He is a good man, or, she is a good woman." This is a byproduct of longsuffering and kindness in your relationships.

The Last Three: Our Personal Development as People

Faithfulness is the first characteristic of these last three fruits. Unlike a person of faith, who has confidence and trust in his or her theology, faithfulness speaks to their ethics and integrity as a person. Will you do what you said you would do? That speaks to one's fidelity or loyalty in life; are you trustworthy; can you be counted on? It is your morality on display, which is your ethics. Our faith controls what we believe, but our faithfulness controls how we behave.

Meekness is one of the most misunderstood characteristics in our society today. It is not weakness, but rather on being gentle from a position of strength; it means to have great power which is always under control. Most police officers live out the true meaning of meekness everyday; Jesus Christ is the most powerful person the world has ever known, yet He was always under control.

Self-control is a characteristic our society could use more development in. It refers to restraining or holding back oneself, to take hold of your life in the realm of anger, lust, gossip, violence, and tardiness. When you have hold of your life through the power of the Holy Spirit, you can be more faithful in your marriage, more productive on your job, more dependable and more rational-thinking as a person.

So as we develop a deeper understanding of God,

His word, and His will on how we are to live in this world, our public response to any form of attack, no matter how psychologically and emotionally painful, will always be correct, holy, and righteous.

The Recipient of the Response

In our society it is a very natural thing to repay someone in kind, meaning you inflict pain on them if they caused you pain. If they brought suffering to your house, you bring it to theirs. We find this doctrine in our attitudes, our media entertainment, and even in our beliefs and politics.

So the doctrine I am about to speak about may seem like a *crazy* one to most in our society, but the concept is simple and the rewards are priceless.

> Recompense to no man evil for evil. Provide things honest in the sight of all men. If it be possible, as much as lieth in you, live peaceably with all men. Dearly beloved, avenge not yourself,

but rather give place unto wrath: for it is written, Vengeance is mine; I will repay saith the Lord. Therefore if thine enemy hunger, feed him, if he thirst give him drink for in so doing thou shalt heap coals of fire on his head. Be not overcome of evil, but overcome evil with good. (Romans 12:17–21).

Beloved the doctrine carries some very deep emotional and psychological opportunities for development in a sinful and rebellious society where most men are enemies to God and to each other. You who are a friend to God must also be friendly to men. Seeking vengeance for one's own reduces us to the level of the animal that has no ability of reason or high consciousness. When vengeance and wrath start to build up in you, let it flow out of you uneventfully. When you allow this then you can repay evil with good publicly, and just like coals of fire can melt away iron so your works of kindness can melt away their evil. The theme of the doctrine is that when you fail to overcome evil you lose, but when you overcome evil with good you have the victory. The doctrine is about maximizing the opportunity of soul winning by evangelizing through behavior and attitude. An example of this behavior would be Christ on the cross when he said "Father forgive them for they know not what they do." The wife who repays adultery with forgiveness, the crime victim who forgives their attacker, the employee who takes the high road in the midst of slander and gossip are all wonderful examples of overcoming evil.

CHAPTER 5

FORMS OF ATTACKS

Having a form of godliness but denying its power and from such people turn away, for of this sort are those who creep into households and make captives of gullible women loaded down with sins lead away by various lusts (2 Timothy 3:5–7).

Outsourcing:

It would be almost impossible to write a book in today's business climate without talking about outsourcing. It is one of the most divisive topics throughout corporate America today. It was a major political issue in the 2012 presidential election between President Barack Obama and candidate Mitt Romney and is a source of attack for many Americans in the corporate environment today. But before we go on, let's identify what outsourcing officially is.

Outsourcing is when one company contracts out a portion of their jobs and/or services to another company on subcontractor. When I was in business, I outsourced my payroll responsibilities to a payroll company; many small businesses follow this same practice. Most small businesses don't have the staff, skill set, technology, or finances to do certain types of needed tasks that are critical to their business operations like printing services, payroll services, bookkeeping services, accounting services, and so on. This type of outsourcing seems okay in the public's mind because most small businesses don't have the staff to perform these functions, and nobody loses their job.

What gives outsourcing a bad name is when large companies, such as Fortune 500 companies, outsource divisions of their companies to subcontractors.

Many credit card companies outsource their customer service divisions to smaller subcontractors overseas in countries like India; many sneaker and shoe companies outsource a portion of their manufacturing services to smaller subcontractors in Asian countries. Many automobile companies outsource divisions of their manufacturing to smaller subcontractors in Mexico. These management decisions are almost always made for financial gains, and these gains almost all come from labor savings in that it is more cost-effective to lay off American workers and replace them with foreign ones. As bad and devastating as this is, the next level of outsourcing can be more psychologically and emotionally devastating.

When Fortune 500 companies and municipalities outsource entire departments and divisions of their managers and employees to private contractors, the problem is that the managers and employees don't lose their jobs; they don't even change work addresses. They just change employment status. So you may say well that's not so bad and it isn't, but we must always go back to the reason for outsourcing and that is increased financial gains.

So let's take a look back at our great republic. America started its financial journey to becoming an economic superpower during the agricultural industry. This was good for the country because of the slave labor. Profits were high and expenses were minimal. As the nation moved into the industrial revolution of manufacturing, profits were still high as expenses were still somewhat minimal, but during the 1920s through the 1940s, labor began to organize and demanded fair, livable wages. This was a good time for labor because skill sets became high. Machinery became complex, and labor operations became extremely expensive. But now, as the nation finds itself moving from the manufacturing industry to the service industry, we find organized labor losing ground to outsourcing because in a service industry the skill set demand is not as high for labor as it was in the industrial manufacturing period.

So when management companies sign contracts to take over departments and or divisions of a corporation, their main objective is to reduce cost for the company. Now this is where this kind of outsourcing earns its bad name. That same employee who does not lose his or her job will lose their job status. They are no longer an employee of their former company even though they are still working at the same location, doing pretty much the same job. The problem with this is: this employee's skill set and company knowledge is being exploited by their new company while they may or may not make the same annual salary, but in most cases they will be paying more out of their paychecks for their healthcare coverage, they will get less vacation time, and their work environment will become more restrictive.

In America today the service industry is geared towards the younger workers; management companies seek out employees who are educated but lack experience. Older workers are more set in their ways and have a manufacturing industry mindset, which is an eight-hour day and then you go home; anything else is overtime pay. This mindset runs counter to the do-more-with-less doctrine the service industry promotes. Younger workers tend to be more idealistic in their approach to a job and career, and they cost less than their older counterparts. Older workers through experience tend to be more practical in their approach to jobs and career and would always like to be compensated for what they feel they are worth. The dynamics of this process carry deep psychological and emotional resentment towards both the outsource company and the former company. It's based on a feeling of betrayal and dishonesty. I linked it to modern-day sharecropping, where you can still stay on the plantation but your status, work environment, and quality of life will drastically change because someone wants to put more money in their pockets. Now, beloved, please don't misunderstand me, these outsourcing or management consultant companies are great companies with salt-of-the-earth employees. I have worked for a few of them in my career, and they are also caught up in this combative, often volatile, environment. Because of this, a lot of these contractual relationships have an average life span of three to five years. And when these contracts end, in most cases, it's the outsource company ending the relationship for lack of payment.

The thief does not come except to steal, and to kill, and to destroy (John 10:10).

For the love of money is a root of all kinds of evil, for which some have strayed from the faith in their greediness, and pierced themselves through with many sorrows (1Timothy 6:10).

Beloved these scriptures describe how many believers in the faith stray from pursuing the daily things of God to pursue money. The Apostle Paul is not calling money evil; money is a blessed gift from God, and you shall "remember the Lord your God for it is He who gives you power to get wealth that He swore to your fathers, as it is this day" (Deuteronomy 8:18).

But the love of money is the character flaw which Paul condemns. "No one can serve two masters, for either he will hate the one and love the other, or else he will be loyal to the one and despise the other. You cannot serve God and mammon" (Matthew 6:24).

So what contributes to this negative psychological and emotional dynamic is the process of the presentation sell. When a contract is signed and all the details are worked out, most if not all management firms come in bearing gifts; the first week there will be free coffee and donuts for everybody, and then the next couple of months there will be quiet observation and polite conversation. This is followed by new upgrades in equipment for what- ever the discipline is, along with new information technology upgrades. After all of this is done, now you are coming up on the first year anniversary of the contract. Then things like unitization and standardization are introduced into the daily workforce.

Unitization: The configuration of smaller units of information into large coordinated units.

This is a methodology for job designing or job creating, building and eight-hour work schedules, one unit at a time.

Standardization: To conform to one standard. All staff will start work at one time and end at another time. All staff will get three weeks of vacation, one hour lunch breaks, and six federal holidays.

As these forms of methodologies are introduced to the workforce, time is being measured, waste must be eliminated, and a resentful feeling of control comes over the employee. Welcome to the doctrine of do more with less. Beloved, now is not the time to fall apart or be torn apart because of what you see or hear. Now is the time for an internal battle, we must learn how to conquer the five kings in our lives. They are our five senses, and we must not allow them to rob us of our future.

How many time has someone ruined their future because of what they heard and acted the wrong way on that information. You heard a rumor about your wife, acted upon it, and got locked up for spousal abuse; you saw a beautiful and attractive young man or woman and lost your marriage because of adultery. You felt like you were disrespected on your job and developed a bad attitude, disrespecting others and got a bad evaluation; you have a sweet tooth and thirty pounds later you are taking high blood pressure medication. Beloved these five senses were given to us by God so we could effectively and accurately interact with the world around us, but we allow them to run rampant in our lives until they become dream killers and joy robbers. Oh no, now is not the time to give an ear to them but to the Holy Spirit and learn about His fruit.

Discipline

My son do not despise the chastening of the Lord,
nor detest His correction, for whom the Lord loves He
corrects, just as a Father the Son in whom He delights
(Proverbs 3:11-12).

Beloved it has been my experience, in over twenty-
nine years in management positions, that most managers
very rarely get disciplined for job performance issues
or aptitude but are more frequently disciplined for
behavior or attitude issues. I believe this comes from
the environment our corporate management psychology
creates. Most corporations still function internally on
a colonial system of titles and subordinate supervision
relationships, and the psychology behind this is, the
greater the title the more power, money, and prestige you
will receive. So a very large part of a manager's career
is spent jockeying and maneuvering for bigger titles and
more money and prestige, and too often the steps used to
reach these heights are on the backs of subordinates and

colleagues. In *The Corporate Christian: Christian Beliefs vs. Corporate Behaviors*, I identified this as a corporation's subculture, which was almost always never seen but always felt by its employees. This combative and unethical environment creates a superficial executive who only wants to look the part but is too afraid to commit to it for fear of making a bad decision or mistake and being torn apart by the vicious subculture. So instead a performance is played out promoting education, knowledge, and a complete air of certainty.

The scripture says "pride goes before destruction and a haughty spirit before a fall" (Proverbs16:18–19).

This kind of pride is personified in an ambitious character who is never satisfied in his or her present state. Money alone can't feed this ambitious pride, which is driven to get power, position, and influence over people and leaves destruction in its wake. It is also accompanied by a haughty or high-minded air of arrogance of spirit. This character walks with head held high and never looks where they are walking. When people get to the height of their riches, power, and prestige and they are really feeling themselves, they are on the precipice of complete ruin.

These type of people refuse to humble them- selves and follow instructions, much less receive correction, so when discipline comes to their door, it's always because of attitude and not aptitude.

The ironic thing about this dynamic is that sound corrective discipline is designed to enhance you and help you through revealing the things we tend not to see about ourselves because of pride and arrogance. "This above all, to thine own self be true, and it must follow, as the night the day, thou can't not then be false to any man" (William Shakespeare).

Politics

In the *Corporate Christian: Christian belief vs. Corporate Behaviors* we briefly touched on this topic. Here allow me to go a little deeper. Politics is the scheming and sly behavior that belongs to cliques or groups during controversial matters. When politics enters the workplace, it always divides people. First and foremost, all politics is premeditated and is always divided among common interests, but more importantly race and ethnicity. People who have common interests, language, race, and or ethnic backgrounds tend to politic together. The big problem with politics is that it entices immorality, and attacks and destroys ethics, which is morality on display. The characteristic of politics are untrustworthiness, slyness, ambitiousness, pride, and ego. Politics ushers hostility in the workplace, creates division, and breeds violence and hatred. It is a very formidable weapon to defend against, but it can be defeated. First do not cultivate cares and deep affections for things of the world. Control all appetites for ambitious gains, and always remember to please God in your behavior before your boss.

Corruption

In most cases politics and corruption are like inseparable twins. They are very hard to separate, and they often operate with the same mind. Politics is the door, and corruption is the reward. Corruption is the deterioration of morality in a person's life for a variety of reasons. The main ones are laziness and impatience. This is when a person is too lazy to work within the practical policies and social rules of an organization and too impatient to work to achieve career success through their own merit and skills. Individuals who often get caught in corruption most of the time will blame the politics of the environment as the main obstacle in their way for career success. These two characteristics should always be avoided for their success is always based on selling an illusion of who they really are, while quickly orchestrating schemes to get what they desire most.

The venom of corruption is so powerful that its infectious symptoms can permanently alter the human character through the destroying of innocence. In the *Corporate Christian*, I expounded upon this dynamic.

Because of the covert nature of corruptive behavior

the Lazy eye often is not aware of its existence and almost always never recognizes it when it is finally revealed.

The trauma of betrayal has become a reality and the lack of trust and a suspicious nature has started to be developed as a defense system to ensure this does not affect or harm us again.

Favoritism

Another very big byproduct of politics, this is unfairly favoring or rewarding persons or groups who supported the sly scheming behavior to bring about the political outcome that "all will eventually benefit from." As I became a Pastor of the St. Mark Missionary Baptist Church, I started to become involved in some political issues on behalf of the community in which I serve. I quickly saw the political machine and system at work, and because I went into activities for purely community reasons, I was quickly ruled out as one who would get any favors. As a matter of fact; most clergy often find themselves on the outside looking in. In these kinds of relationships the ones who benefit often close their eyes to any immoral behavior. This weapon can reap devastating damage on us as workers and Christians. When those who have rule over us exercise favoritism around us and leave us feeling like we are on the outside looking in, our productivity and morale can go on life support. We develop strong mistrust issues among our co-workers, and arguments can become the norm in the workplace.

Beloved, once again know who you are and whose you are, "But you are a chosen generation, a royal priesthood, a holy nation, His own special people that may proclaim the praises of Him who called you out of darkness into His marvelous light" (1 Peter 2:9).

You have already been chosen by God for a special work that will get done without and in spite of man's politics, corruption, and favoritism. So don't dare change who you are for anyone who operates in these unethical systems, "Let the favor of the Lord our God be upon us and establish the work of our hands upon us; yes establish the work of our hands" (Psalm 90:17). Only through God can your life have value, significance, meaning, clarity, and direction.

CHAPTER 6

DON'T LOVE THE THINGS YOUR JOB PROVIDES

Do not love the world or the things in the world; if anyone loves the world, the love of the Father is not in him (1 John 2:15).

A foundational principle to getting the victory in the battle for your beliefs is to reject any deep affection in your heart for the world. Now allow me to expand on this concept. It's a known fact that the things you care about the most can be used to control and enslave you, so when the scriptures say not to love the world or the things in the world, it is laying down a doctrine for our ultimate protection.

The World

When the scriptures refer to the world, what it is not referring to is the physical material world all around us, but rather the invisible spiritual system of evil that is controlled and dominated by Satan and all of its opposition to God, His word, and His people.

Love: In this context, the word *love* is referring to affection and devotion. Where will your heart's affections and devotions lie? Here is the complexity of this doctrine: God is a God of love and love is the most dominant part of His character for by it salvation was offered. "God so loved the world that He gave His only begotten Son that whosoever believeth in Him should not perish but have ever- lasting life" (John 3:16).

He is also asking that His love be a dominant part of our character—but for people, not for the things in which they believe that are contrary to Him. So do not love the world system that has been designed to set men against each other to promote ego and self and fulfill the three windows of rebellion: "For all that is in the world, the lust of the flesh, the lust of the eyes, and the pride of life is not of the Father but is the world" (1 John 2:16).

Beloved, the world system says people are designed for and orchestrated to interact with and respond to their surroundings (the things of the world) and each other on the basis of how they feel about it: what it looks like to them and what can it do for them. The world's system makes decisions according to its natural fleshly senses. This process is wrapped in philosophies and ideologies that give the appearance of attractiveness and sound common sense, but it is evil in its motivation for it is designed to serve the one and not the whole equally. Let me break this down a little more.

The Lust of the Flesh: The rebellious, self-dominated nature that is always in opposition to Gods word. Romans 7:15–19 says,

For what I am doing, I do not understand. For what I will to do, that I do not practice, but what I hate, that I do. If then, I do what I will not to do, I agree with the law that it is good. But now, it is no longer I who do it but sin that dwells in me. For I know that in me (that is in my flesh) nothing good dwells; for to will is present with me, but to perform what is good I do not find. For the good that I will to do, I do not do; but the evil I will not to do that I practice.

The world system is used to incite our flesh, or better yet, the sin nature is our flesh.

The Lust of the Eyes: The pathways to stir up the wrong desires in our hearts or wills. Eve was lured away by something attractive and beautiful. "So when the woman saw that the tree was good for food, that it was pleasant to the eyes and a tree desirable to make one wise, she took of its fruit and ate. She also gave to her husband with her and he ate" (Genesis 3:6).

The Pride of Life: The arrogance of man in the corporate environment over his circumstances and affairs. This mindset and attitude produces haughty behavior, exaggerations, embellishments, parading and exhibiting possessions, positions, and accomplishments to impress others. "But now you boast in your arrogance all such boasting is evil. Therefore to him who knows to do good and does not do it, to him it is sin" (James 4:16–17).

When people boast and brag about anticipated accomplishments, they will always try to ensure the outcome is in their favor to support their boasting. So they will do things that they should not be doing. Their sins of omission lead directly to their sins of commission.

Enslavement

Jesus answered them, "most assuredly I say to you, whoever commits sin is a slave of sin and a slave does not abide in the house forever, but a son abides forever. Therefore if the son makes you free, you shall be free indeed (John 8:34–36).

Beloved, even though we live in a free society there are a lot of enslaved folk who are working and living among us. I am not talking about physical slavery but rather habitual and addictive slavery, slaves to rebellious and immoral behavior (sin) which they cannot control but rather are being controlled by.

Let me explore this a little further. The Bible teaches that sinful and rebellious behavior is very addicting behavior and becomes bad habitual behavior. What makes this issue so potent in a person's life is that it comes through those three windows I talked about in the last chapter.

Its potency is in its naturalness and familiarity to your flesh or natural human nature. You see, beloved, when you respond to the outside stimuli of the world based on what you see, what you hear, or what you want, it feels right and good. The problem with this is that we don't live on an island by ourselves, and what feels right to me will almost certainly not feel so right to my co-worker. This is the essence of rebellious behavior: it's really selfish and immature behavior, and immature folk are the easiest to enslave because they live by the, me-first doctrine all the time.

Now I want to be very clear on what is being talked about here. All people sin, including all Christians, but what Christ is specifically speaking to and about is the habitual practice of selfish, immature, rebellious, immoral behavior which is the norm of an individual's life, where it is not the unbroken pattern of the Christian's life.

Let's look at some very dangerous hurtful rebellious behavior that feels good to the immature and selfish person:

- Adultery—A voluntary violation of the marriage bed by one spouse
- Infidelity—Unfaithfulness, disloyalty
- Gossip—Idle talk or rumor, especially about the personal or private affairs of others
- Envy—Feelings of dissatisfaction or covetousness

Don't Love the Things Your Job Provides

with regards to another's advantages, success, or possessions

- Drunkenness—Intoxicated, quarrelsome, loud, disruptive

These are just a few behaviors that enslave the selfish and immature mind. They all come through our three windows and feel good to our natural nature.

Let's take a closer look at these behaviors and see if we can trace their beginnings and endings.

The act of committing adultery with a co-worker can be an extremely dangerous decision. We said that adultery is a voluntary violation of the marriage bed by one person in a marriage, and because this type of behavior is so hurtful and painful to the other party or parties, we never get down to the level in a person where this rebellion starts So a plan of defense can be implemented and the behavior adverted before it takes root.

A significant amount of adulterous affairs happen

99

between co-workers, meaning that a place where the Almighty blessed you and placed you for provision for your family has now become a place of pain and destruction for the family because of selfish, immature immoral, rebellious behavior. This type of behavior is first and foremost ego-driven.

It simultaneously opens our windows in this order: first, the pride of life for this type of adultery will require premeditated pursuing, second the lust of the eyes in which the prey must always look beautiful and attractive to be worth the effort, and third, the lust of the flesh. The closer we get to the desired outcome, the hotter the flesh burns.

This systematic attack on your behavior, character reputation, and soul is the basic design for all enslaving behaviors; I love the Apostle Paul's climatic ending in Romans chapter seven. In his ending he is able to draw the picture of the human experience for both believer and non-believer along with a real self-portrait of whom we are:

I find then a law, that evil is present with me, the one who wills to do good. For I delight in the law of God according to the inward man. But I see another law in my members, war- ring against the law of my mind, and bringing me into captivity to the law of sin/rebellion which is in my members. Oh wretched man that I am! Who will deliver me from this body of death? I thank God through Jesus Christ our Lord! So then with my mind, I myself serve the law of God, but with the flesh the law of sin (Romans 7:21-25).

The translation is, I recognize that I am very capable of evil behavior and thoughts even when I am willing and wanting to do well. So I will delight in and focus on the good law of God with all of my thoughts while my natural nature wars against the thoughts of my mind and from time to time make me respond to the world in a sinful and rebellious manner. I can't do what I would like to do all the time; I hate this war that is in me and need some- body to free me from this contradiction of belief and behavior. Thank God through Christ who has given me a new mind and perspective that I am no longer under the control of the old unredeemed mind that walked hand-in-hand with my old nature. Now understand what is being said: old ways and habits are hard to break and become a natural way of life until one learns a new way, but one must always accept responsibility for all behavior. We can never use the Flip Wilson's character Geraldine, who always blamed the devil, "the devil made me do it." Paul is saying that the new law of God which the new mind has a strong desire to follow and *obey* must be developed so it can have complete control of your entire nature and humanness. When we do fall there is no condemnation applied to us for Jesus paid it all and freed us from any penalty of past, present, or future rebellious behavior. So to overcome this kind of attack, one must have the right mind, this mind which was also in Christ Jesus (Philippians 2:5). You see, God is a mind regulator in that He controls your thought (if you let Him). He is a mind alternator: He keeps your mind just right, never too hot or too cold, He is a mind saturator in that He keeps pouring into you, and He is a mind adjuster carrying you from faith to faith and to new levels of maturity in Him so you can be truly free.

Living Free

There is therefore now, no condemnation to those who are in Christ Jesus, who do not walk according to the flesh but according to the spirit. For the law of the spirit of life in Christ Jesus has made me free from the law of sin and death (Romans 8:2).

As a nation we are made up of immigrants, all of us originated from someplace else; a lot of us were brought here with evil intention, while a lot came for a better way of life. All of our ancestors were baptized in the fire of trials and tribulation and had to fight to carve out a nation in this vast blessed wilderness.

Daniel Webster in 1820 stood at Plymouth Rock for the nation's 200-year celebration and said this, "let us not forget the religious character of our origins. Our fathers were brought here by their high veneration for the Christian religion, they journeyed by its light and labored in it hope. They sought to incorporate its principles with the elements of their society and to diffuse is influence through all their institutions, civil, political or literary."

As a nation and society we strayed from righteousness through the cursed institutions of slavery and Jim Crow, and now we find ourselves straying even further through corruption, manipulation, intimidation, and domination in our political and corporate leadership. Oh wretched nation, who can deliver us from this?

My good friend and fellow author Cheryl Wills of the book *Die Free* has an opinion of which I am in agreement with, and that is if African Americans only truly knew what life was really like for our ancestors, our behavior would be quite different. If we could connect the dots that at one time this country (America) legally forbade us from learning to read, write, and pursue an education and if caught we would be mutilated or killed. So why are we now, with free public education, the lowest performers in the nation? If we only truly new what life was like for the black man and woman, certainly black-on-black crime and black domestic violence and rape would be at an all-time low in our communities.

Beloved, free living only comes from the true knowledge of who you are and whose we are. Political corruption of our elected officials at the national, regional, and local levels could be drastically reduced if our leaders truly understood what it took to get here and build this nation from the common man's perspective.

CHAPTER 7

LEADERSHIP

The elders who are among you I exhort, I who am a fellow elder and a witness of the sufferings of Christ, and also a partaker of the glory that will be revealed: shepherd the flock of God which is among you, serving, as overseers, not by compulsion but willingly, not for dishonest gain but eagerly; nor as being lords over those entrusted to you, but being examples to the flock (1 Peter 5:1–4).

Tone and Atmosphere

The tone in which our corporate leaders lead and the atmosphere it creates is the foundation of why you have to battle for your beliefs in the corporate environment. They are the spark and fuel that sustain a very hostile working environment.

The American society today is a very impatient one, and most American workers don't have a lot of tolerance for being addressed in aggressive and authoritative tones in a toxic and combustible atmosphere. And leaders who are not sensitive to the tone and atmosphere in their companies create big problems for those companies: problems such as high employee turnover, high sick-time abuse, and low productive performance by the workforce. All of these things combined can cripple an organization.

The Apostle Peter gives a wonderful blueprint on how to lead, especially in a highly competitive, highly stressful environment. It's based on one doctrine that should become a way of life for leaders. They are elation and elevation or the doctrine of exhorting.

To exhort someone means to *earnestly* urge and advise. So executive leadership should always be earnestly urging and advising middle and frontline leadership on how they expect them to lead the workforce. In these times of great stress, worry, depression, politics, and corruption in our corporations, now is the best time for the most noblest of leaders who know how to and when to exhort the staff. We cannot say exhort them and leave it at that. Let's follow the Apostle Peters example.

He says, to leadership "The elders who are among you I exhort or advise; I who am a fellow elder and a witness of the suffering of Christ. This is motivation through identification, when the president or vice president identifies themselves with you as a manager and can relate to what you are dealing with that's a pretty good motivator. He tells them I Peter, who personally witnessed Christ suffering, am an elder just like you. Once he gets their attention, then he starts to strongly advise them. His exhortation message covers three points:

1. Who are we: we serve as the overseers for Gods flock.
2. What is our primary role: we are called to feed and protect the flock. This is done by teaching; every leader must know how to teach. Also, we must be watchful to recognize wolves, disgruntled sheep, and bad habits and behaviors.
3. How do we do this: This should never be done by compulsion but willingly, never for dishonest gain but eagerly and never as being lords over those entrusted to you but rather be an example?

So leadership should always be present and seen, with fewer meetings and more presence; willing to teach and instruct whenever necessary they should also be present to recognize any problems that might arise and be ready to protect and defend the staff with clear resolutions. This must be done in a very specific way because our goal is to keep a watchful eye on the tone and atmosphere of the environment. So the above performance of leadership should never be done due to being compelled to do it. Compulsion takes all the joy out of the performance as compared to doing it willingly, and because you want to do it, in this performance there is joy evermore. There is a saying that goes something like this. "When you are doing what you want to do, you'll never work another day in your life."

When the work is done out of compulsion, leaders do the work in laziness and forget the urgency and importance of the task.

Each of you should give what you have decided in your heart to give, not reluctantly or under compulsion, for God loves a cheerful giver (2 Corinthians 9:7)

Laziness and indifference take the joy out of any environment, and this is also true for financial motivation: money is never a good reason to commit to anything. It only leads to wanting more, which can lead to corruption. Finally, when leading and managing folks, never do it by lording over them; in other words never let you leadership be done through manipulation, intimidation, or domination. If you want people to follow you lead them by example. Always be ready to set the example for them to follow.

The Problem of the Workplace

In this the children of God and the children of the devil are manifest. Whoever does not practice righteousness is not of God nor is he who does not love his brother (1 John 3:10).

I believe the main problem with the workplace today is the lack of right living or righteousness and love for our fellow man. We bear witness to it through the toxic corporate environments where corporations gamble and lose senior employees' pensions, when jobs are eliminated and shipped overseas to make a buck for investors, when the do-more-with-less doctrine becomes a reality and hostility and combativeness become part of the daily environment, when outsourcing is introduced because upper management is unwilling or unable to develop its staff for the future.

Yes, we do have a big problem in our corporations today, and it starts with our leadership. In most of our Fortune 500 companies, the average executive is making conservatively three times more than their middle management counterparts and at least four times what their front-line managers are making. This is at a base salary level and not including over- time. If the average salaries for middle managers range from sixty-five thousand to one hundred ten thousand dollars per year, then their executive leadership is averaging in a range from one hundred ninety-six thousand to three hundred thirty thousand dollars per year. In today's society, executives who are making these kinds of salaries and more need to be careful of falling into the trap of feeling that they are worth every dollar of these salaries. This kind of thinking opens the window to the pride of life where bragging and self-promotion lives. You, at the executive level, this is not part of your job duties for your leadership should always be by example and symbolic. You represent the highest standard of work ethics in your companies and when your staff sees you they should think of that standard.

Delegation and Span of Control: The Moses Story

Moses' father-in-law said to him, "The thing that you do is not good. Both you and these people who are with you will surely wear yourselves out. For this thing is too much for you; you are not able to perform it by yourself (Exodus 18:17–18).

This man Moses had a fascinating life story that all generations can learn and benefit from, even in today's fast-pace world.

Born into slavery by heritage and ethnicity, he was adopted by the most powerful man in Egypt, Pharaoh's, daughter and as a future Prince of Egypt it was expected that he be learned and skilled in military strategy, construction projects, finances, inventory control, and diplomacy. Now you all know the story, so I won't go into all of it, but I do want to continue on with this remarkable piece of advice given to him. Jethro, Moses' father-in-law, said to him:

Listen now to my voice, I will give you counsel and God will be with you: stand before God for the people, so that you may bring the difficulties to God. And you shall teach them the way in which they most walk and the work they must do. More over you shall select from all the people able man, such as fear God men of truth, hating covetousness and place such over them to be rulers of thousands, rulers of hundreds, rulers of fifties and rulers of tens. And let them judge the people at all times. Then it will be that every great matter they shall bring to you, but every small matter they themselves shall judge. So it will be easier for you, for they will bear the burden with you (Exodus 18:19-22).

This counsel from Jethro is full of practical wisdom and spiritual insight that make it a perfect combination for success. First, Jethro instructed Moses to stand before God for the people and bring the difficulties to God: The foundation of great leadership is servitude; you are there to serve first—and not to be served first. Second, it is leadership's primary responsibility to teach and develop the people and show them exactly what is expected of them when they are given this gift of knowledge and wisdom, which is the application of knowledge. Third, you must select from all the people not just the rich, the white, the black, and the good-looking but from all the people: men of truth, of strong moral and ethical standards, who hate covetousness, who are not envious and jealous petty folk. Jethro told Moses to pick them by the content of their character and not just by the color of their skin, their last name, or who they knew. Last, span of control assures the proper ratio of rulers to people based on the skills of each class of ruler.

Once Moses understood this, in other words, once he was able to lay down his extensive resume and litany of accomplishments, he stopped being the bottleneck problem and became the great, great leader as we know him today. Once Jethro's advice was received and implemented, the Ten Commandments were given to the people.

Moses then wrote the laws of the altar, laws concerning servants, laws concerning violence, laws for animal control and the responsibility for property, moral principles and justice for all, and the law concerning the Sabbath. The design for the Ark of the Covenant and the portable Tabernacle were drafted and the Promised Land was surveyed and divided.

Beloved, in other words Moses, through Jethro's counsel, developed the leadership and the people to take and live in the Promised Land. Preparation should never start when you arrive at your destination but rather long before you even know where you are going to be; anything else will only create chaos and confusion.

CHAPTER 8

UNITY

Now I am no longer in the world, but these are in the world, and I come to you. Holy Father keep through your name those whom you have given me that they may be one as we are one (John 17:11).

The Oxford American dictionary says that unity is oneness being one, single or individual being formed of parts that constitute a whole.

Why is unity so important in any group activity, why do nations, corporations, sports teams, and yes even animals depend so much on it? What are its secrets and power? Can anything stand up to a unified front? Why did the Son of God pray to the Father that we and His disciples be kept united as one?

Well, beloved, from a physical standpoint we know that one strand of thread can break but not even a strong man can break ten thousand strands of thread woven together.

Strength: So we know that in unity there is strength. A herd of elephants, a pride of lions, and a swarm of bees are all very powerful and frightening forces to stand against. How could one chase a thousand, and two put ten thousand to flight, unless their Rock had sold them, and the Lord has surrendered them? (Deuteronomy 33:30).

Security and Safety: There is also security and safety in unity; there is great safety in numbers. A great united force is also a powerful deterrent to any sinister, aggressive behavior.

Peace: Unity is a foundational building block for peace; Can two walk together, except they be agreed? (Amos 3:3)

Productivity: When people are united, they are very productive. The Lord said in Genesis 11:6, "Indeed the people are one and they all have one language, and this is what they begin to do: now nothing that they propose to do will be withheld from them."

So you see, beloved, whether you are building a ministry, a nation, or a company, if you have people in there, you will need to have unity for success.

When a corporation is united it displays strength in its workforce, its service, attitude, and brand. When we look at companies like Pan American Airline of the 1940s, 50s, 60s and 70s, Ford Motors of the 1960s and 70s, and Microsoft and IBM of the 1980s and 90s, we see that they portray unified fronts of strength, which translated in big, robust profits that were shared by all.

This also brought them and their employee's great job security and safety for a number of decades.

Unity also breeds camaraderie, brotherhood and sisterhood, when a group feels like they are in it together—if they survive all of them survive and if they go down, they all go down. When this ideology is present, any kind of challenge or obstacle will always unify the group or body. So why is it so hard to unite a company?

Disunity

In the *Corporate Christian,* I touched on this topic briefly from a dissenting behavior standpoint and the challenges disunity creates for unity in the corporate environment. In this chapter let us approach it from the sinfulness of man and his natural nature and why it is such a challenge to create and keep a group united in society today.

THE CORPORATE CHRISTIAN: BOOK 2

These six things the Lord hates, yes seven are an abomination to Him: A proud look, a lying tongue, hands that shed innocent blood, a heart that devises wicked plans, feet that are swift in running to evil, a false witness who speaks lies and one who sows discord among brethren. (Proverbs 6:16–19).

In our sinful nature we have a propensity for wickedness in any setting especially in intense, high-stress, competitive environments. These types of environments bring out these types of behaviors from us and disrupt and even sometimes derail all unifying efforts. Wicked people are really worthless folk who cause more damage than they are worth, for their lives are consumed with perverse mouths that tell all kinds of gossip and lies, having haughty and flirtatious eyes which are stuck on themselves, swift and shuffling feet that go after evil desires and behaviors, and hands that always destroy the innocent and unsuspecting.

Depravity and perversity are continually in their hearts to turn people against each other for political and or financial gain.

It is very difficult for a company's policies and procedure to address this kind of heart and or behavior. So most people fight this kind of fire with their own version of it until you have a raging inferno at the workplace, and no one is able to put it out.

The effects of disunity in the workplace are disastrous and profound. A divided workforce is a very weak unproductive, out-of-synch, chaotic workforce. People are divided, and in most cases they are divided on common ground. A big common ground is:

Race

Now I am no longer in the world, but these are in the world, and I come to you. Holy Father keep through your name those whom you have given me, that they maybe one as we are (John 17:11).

Jesus' prayer was not just a wish for Him but a

foundational part of the Christian faith. For He knew the potential for danger that disunity would have among the body

They tell me that the most segregated hour in America today is still Sunday morning. When most races and ethnic groups go to their own churches of likeness, praying to the same God and believing in the same spirit with hope in the same Son, it is practiced among people who look like us, and we premeditatedly violate the prayer of the Master because we cannot unite.

Race does not only divide us in church, it divides us in the neighborhoods we live in, the schools we send our children to, the places we socialize in, and the people we socialize with—of which I am also guilty. So how do our corporations even stand a chance to correct this if we as people are unable or unwilling to do so ourselves?

Ethnicity

The United States of America is one of the world's

most ethnically diverse and multicultural nations on the planet. This is the result of large- scale immigration to America from many countries. The main ethnic groups in America today are Europeans, Africans, Latin Americans, Asians and Native Americans, and within these groups are a lot more culturally divided groups. Every person in every group is competing for the same thing: more money for better way of life for themselves and their families—and in our competitive society may the best man win.

A Solution

His Lord said to Him, well done good and faithful servant you have been faithful over a few things, I will make you ruler over many things. Enter into the joy of your Lord (Matthew 25:23).

Beloved, in this scripture lays the solution to resist the individualism that divides us as people in our neighborhoods, cities, states, country, and on our jobs, it can be a great assistance in our battle for our belief while benefitting our corporations internally.

This scripture is about a reward that a certain master gives His servants for being a good steward over His possessions while He was away.

A certain master was leaving for a long journey and He went to three of His servants and gave each of them a certain amount of talents, or money. Upon His return, one of the servants who were given five talents was able to invest it and double it and get ten talents, the servant who was given two talents was able to do the same thing and get back four talents.

They both were also able to get the same rewards, while one was able to bring in six more talents than the other servant they both received the same reward, indicating that the reward from the Master was never for results but rather for faithfulness.

You see, beloved, in the realm of human existence, faith is theological and has to do with what you believe. But faithfulness is ethical and has to do with how you behave. When you find yourself in self-imposed segregation, be faithful to Christ and reach for inclusiveness and diversity; when you find yourself in vicious competition, be faithful to Christ and lend a helping hand. You may just find out that attitudes will always trump aptitudes, and faithfulness will always lead to some kind of fruitfulness.

CHAPTER 9

FORGIVENESS

Then Jesus said, "Father forgive them for they do not know what they do". And they parted His raiment, and cast lots (Luke 23:34).

The Oxford dictionary states that to forgive is first a verb and is the ceasing to feel angry or resentful towards, to pardon.

Forgiveness

The first thing you must always remember when you are in a battle is to never take it personal because personal feelings lead to misguided decisions. When Christ forgave both Roman and Jew at the cross, it was from a sincere belief that they truly did not know what they were doing. They knew they were torturing and beating a man to his death; they knew they schemed, lied, and falsely accused Him. But in spite of all that they were doing, Christ knew that if they truly knew better, their motivations of envy, jealousy, greed, politics, and corruption would not stand a chance.

Beloved, if people truly believed that one day there would be an accounting for all behavior, a reckoning for all actions, violence would almost cease from the earth. Well this is the beginning of righteousness or right living, and it is motivated by the gospel message, which is demanded of us by our Lord and Savior Jesus Christ. It works something like this. The world benefits because of our belief in Christ; we live better, treat each other better, and we benefit because of Christ's belief in us, giving us His salvation, sanctification, and glorification.

So where does forgiveness come from? Well, it comes from the love of God in your life. If you take things personal all the time on your job, you are probably perceiving and receiving things by way of your sight, your hearing, and your emotions or feelings. This is carnal thinking and sowing to the flesh; forgiveness can never be found in this kind of person, only misguided and vengeful thoughts and behaviors. If you are that person who makes sound decisions according to the spirit of God, you are now sowing to the Spirit and scripture says this about both: "For he who sows to his flesh will of the flesh reap corruption, but he who sows to the spirit will of the spirit reap everlasting life" (Galatians 6:8). This means that following your fleshly senses will always lead us into corruptive behavior and situations, but sound spirit-led decisions always lead to life. Allow me a few more minutes to explore this process.

The Workings of Our Humanness

Scripture teaches that man is made of a physical body that is under the control of his mind and in his mind there is a:

Soul: The seat of all human motivations feelings and emotions

Heart: The nature and will of the man

Spirit: The governing authority of the mind

In the unsaved or unredeemed man, this process will work something like this. Worldly outside stimuli in the form of gossip, lust, or desires will bombard the soul, the seat of all human motivations, feeling, and emotions. The heart, which is the natural nature or personality and the will of man, takes the lead and makes the decisions for the body, soul, and spirit on what stimuli they will respond to and how they will respond. The reason why this is a faulty process is because the heart is the most vulnerable of the three to worldly stimuli and can always be enticed, manipulated, and or fooled because it responds on what it sees, hears, or feels. All of these natural senses can be deceived. As it was mentioned earlier in chapter six, do not love the world or the things in the world. "If anyone loves the world, the love of the Father is not in him" (1 John 2:15).

Beloved if the cares and affections for the world and the things of the world are in your heart nature and will, they will choke the love of the Father right out of you. So how do the unredeemed get a foothold on true forgiveness? Well, it's very simple: get redeemed and saved. How do the redeemed get a foothold on forgiveness? This is even simpler. Study the Bible to show yourself approved, beloved; spiritual application can never go before spiritual knowledge, you must know better before you can do better.

Overcoming Our Weakness

We have covered a lot of ground in retrospect on how

to recognize and prepare for these battles that you will surely face in the workplace, but be not dismayed, these internal battles are not germane to Christians, male or females. All of us will have to fight for our peace, our sanity, our characters, our integrity, and even our livelihoods. So allow me to equip you for *battle* that you may overcome your own weakness.

> Therefore take up the whole armor of God, that you may be able to withstand in the evil day, and having done all to stand, stand therefore, having girded your waist with truth, having put on the breast plate of righteousness and having shod your feet with the preparation of the gospel of peace; above all, taking the shield of faith with which you will be able to quench all the fiery darts of the wicked one. And take the helmet of salvation and the sword of the spirit, which is the word of God (Ephesians 6:13–18).

If you are going into the *battle*, the first thing one must do is prepare for battle and the first step in preparation is to make sure you have the right equipment. This is why we are instructed to take up the whole armor of God, not some of it, but rather all of it. Understand that this is not offensive armor but rather defensive so you may be able to stand strong and long in the evil days of attack. To be able to do this, you must stand this way: notice the armor is divided into two groups of three with each one for a specific purpose in this kind of covert espionage. Spiritual warfare will be fought first on the inside of you.

The Armor

The Belt of Truth is to tie down or hold down any loose emotions and or feelings that are worn on our sleeves or backs so lies can't get a hold onto them and pull you off balance. Satan is the father of lies, and he will try to carpet bomb you with them.

The Breastplate of Righteousness: Your righteousness

or right living needs to emulate Christ so when the enemy sees you, they see Him. This breastplate keeps you focused so you are not fooled or enticed by Satan and his schemes to make your belief and behavior not agree.

The Shoes of Peace: Even though you are in a battle, with the shoes of peace wherever you plant your feet you are standing on peaceful solid ground, so you can strand strong and long.

The Shield of Faith: is absolute trust and confidence in God, His word, and His promises so you are not led away by desires and temptation of pleasure that entices the flesh and lures you off the high standard of living and pulls you down into the valley of depravity and despair.

The Helmet of Salvation: prevents you from being traumatized or wounded by the bombs of doubt and discouragement that are launched at us through the trials of life, such as physical sickness, unemployment, job loss, and divorce.

The Sword of the Spirit: is the Word of God and the Truth of the scriptures. It is both our defensive and offensive weapon. It is the only one you will ever need in this battle.

When Christ was in the wilderness fasting for forty days and forty nights, Satan came to Him at His most weak and vulnerable physical state. But because the battle is fought not with or against flesh and blood, He was able to stand boldly and use the sword of the spirit to fend off the attacks.

The First Attack

"If or since you are the Son of God, command that these stones become bread." This was designed to get Him to violate the divine plan.

The Response

"It is written, man shall not live by bread alone, but by every word that proceeds from the mouth of God." God will allow you to hunger, so He can feed you with manna and you may learn to trust and depend on Him during the tough and trying times of life.

The Second Attack

"If or since you are the Son of God, throw yourself down. For it is written: "He shall give His angels charge over you." And, "In their hands they shall bear you up, lest you dash your foot against a stone." This was designed to twist the scriptures and concept of trusting God to testing God, which really doubts Him.

The Response:

"It is written again, you shall not tempt the Lord your God." In our society today we say things like trust but verify, marry but get a prenuptial agreement. This is the concept of doubting under the cover of trust.

The Third Attack

"All these things I will give you if you will fall down and worship me." This is why we are asked not to love the world for Satan is the ruler of this world and the god of this age and everything the eye sees lies in his power for a time.

The Response:

"Away with you Satan for it is written you shall worship the Lord your God and Him only you shall serve." The last response was an offensive one to destroy the strategy of the evil one.

So you see, beloved, only with this specially prepared armor can one truly be ready to overcome human weakness and usher in God's love in our hearts and manifest an attitude of forgiveness.

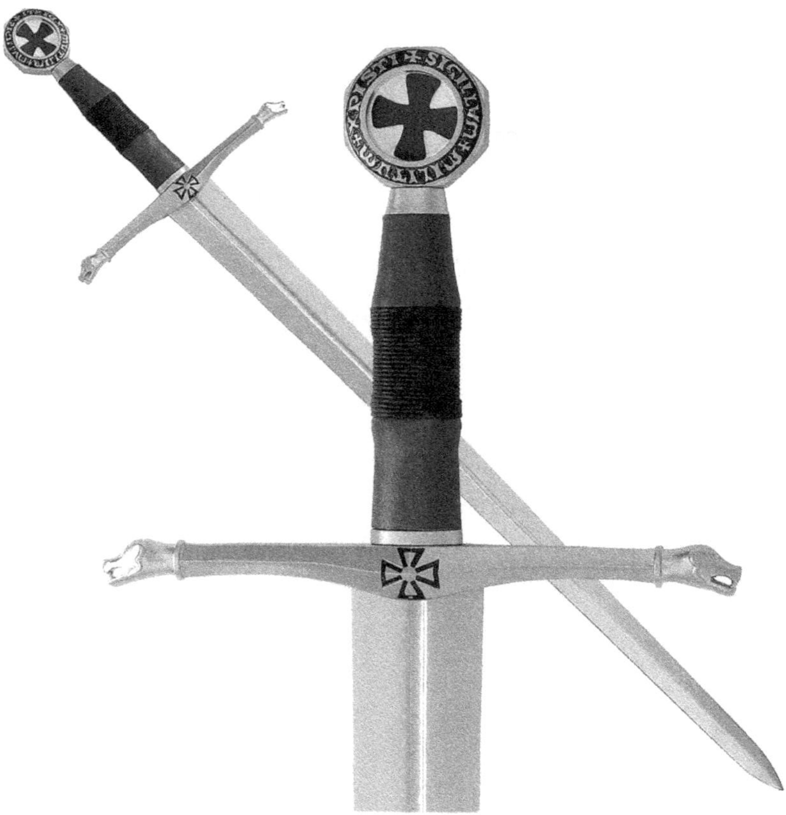

CHAPTER 10

IDENTIFYING THE REAL SNAKES

But when Paul had gathered a bundle of sticks and laid them on the fire a viper came out because of the heat and fastened on his hand. So when the natives saw the creature hanging from his hand they said to one another, "no doubt this man is a murderer, whom, thought he has escaped the sea. Yet justice does not allow to live," But he shook off the creature into the fire and suffered no harm (Act 28:3–5).

First Bite

Beloved, in these scriptures we see the apostle barely surviving a terrible shipwreck from a powerful storm. After being in the waters for hours they finally make it to land, wet, weary, and exhausted where the natives were very kind to them. Now as Paul put wood on the fire, a venomous snake springs from the log he put in the fire and fastens to his hand, and he calmly shakes it off back into the fire,

This would be classified as an unexpected attack, something coming out of nowhere to cause you harm and disrupt the normalcy of life, but the apostle was so focused that he just shook the problem off and went on doing his business. The interesting thing about this scene is the natives and their reaction to this event. My mother, God rest her soul, used to say these old-time sayings around our house. She would always say, "Boy every closed eye isn't sleep, every goodbye isn't gone, and every hello isn't friendly." I never really understood her until I got older and encountered my own snakes.

Second Bite

These natives from this island called Malta greeted them so graciously and kind that it's quite a shock that nobody rushed to help him when the snake bit him. Nobody offered any kind of first aid, but rather when they saw the creature hanging from his hand, they started to gossip among themselves about his situation, his past, and his relationship with God.

There are people out there who will stand afar off and watch you go through your situation while they talk about you, judge you, and expect the worst for you. In Paul's case after they made assumptions about him, they stood and watched for a long time, waiting to see if he would swell up and die—and still they offered no help. Where does this kind of indifference come from? Am I so glad that it was not me that I am willing to rejoice when it's the next person? What does it benefit us to not at least com- fort our brother or sister who is in mourning? When you have been attacked unexpectedly and can't expect support from the crowd, follow the Apostle Paul's advice and shake off the attack immediately. Don't allow the attack and the trauma of it to hang on to you and continue to inject venom into your heart, your mind, your emotions, and your perspectives. Because venom can turn a healthy heart into a mean and evil "Why me" heart, it can turn a sound mind into an indecisive mind, fearful of making any kind of decision. It can turn warm, friendly em tions into cold, callus unsympathetic emotion and a bright positive perspective into a jaded, gloomy, depressed one.

The Anti-Venom

Venom kills our hope and robs us of our future. So how can we defend ourselves? Remember the words of our Lord, "For I know the thoughts that I think towards you, says the Lord, thoughts of peace and not of evil, to give you a future and a hope" (Jeremiah 29:11).

Beloved, this scripture is at the end of a series

beginning at verse five on how to live in difficult situations. You see beloved the Israelites were in a very tough spot. The imperialistic superpower Babylon and their ruthless leader, King Nebuchadnezzar, completely obliterated their way of life and their faith in God. So after many prophets stopping by to tell them what they wanted to hear but not what they needed to hear, God stepped in and spoke to them through the prophet Jeremiah, and he basically said something like this: I know you are in a difficult spot right now, but I want you to get used to it because you are going to be there for a while, and I want you to start enjoying life: buy a house, have some kids, raise them up and marry them off so you may increase and not diminish and wither away. Then I want you to seek the peace of this difficult city that you don't want to be in and pray to the Lord for it because in its peace you will, in return, have peace. Don't let your friends deceive you or lead you astray right now, for it's easy to do while your mind is in a vulnerable state. Don't let them give you false hope

THE CORPORATE CHRISTIAN: BOOK 2

that will never come and only keep the wound open and infected. You will only be here for a season, and there are things for you to do in this season.

Beloved, when things go wrong on the job, when you are disciplined, demoted, transferred to another department or office in a different part of the city or another shift, and the normalcy of your life has been blown apart, how do you handle it? Be very careful on your choices because one wrong move can send everything to hell in a hand basket very quickly. Take a minute to breathe and relax by yourself; now is not the time to be around folks who will be giving you wrong counsel, and remember the words from the prophet. "For I know the thoughts that I think towards you, says the Lord, thoughts of peace and not evil to give you a future and a hope." So when it looks like there is no hope, God said there is hope; when you can't see any good end in sight, God said you will have a future. All you have to do is take your mind off of the trauma because you will be there for a while, so shake it off and continue to live your life, get married, have some kids, go on vacation with the family, do some home repairs, live and enjoy your life for you will have a future. Beloved, in this process God strengthens you spiritually while at the same time he is humbling your character. One who can accept life on life terms and not lose their head is a very humble person.

Healing

So when the bottom falls out publicly and the climax of the show is your demise, this is what the audience, your so-called work friends, are expecting. They are all venomous snakes, and when they bite, a clear sign of venom taking affect in the body is wiggling around in a disoriented state, but, beloved, you are not disoriented. You have a clear goal with a hope and a future, and that is to trust God—believing God in spite of the great number of snakes whispering to one another, expecting for you to fall down and die spiritually, emotionally, psychology, and financially.

One of the most Powerful words to ever be penned on paper is Romans 4:17–18:

> As it is written, I have made thee a father of many nations," in the presence of Him whom he believed, God, who gives life to the dead and calls those things which do not exist as though they were, who against hope believed in hope, that he might become the father of many nations, according to that which was spoken, so shall your descendants be.

This kind of hope produces faith and faith produces God's willpower in your life, so you can stand when you want to lie down, you can walk in, when you want to run out. This is your healing medicine: to be able to see past the trauma, see past all the naysayers, see past self doubt, see past anger and hurt feelings, and see past embarrassment and shame. This is truly Soul Food!

I have come to know through my own personal

experience and three decades of observations that the believer who has a well-prepared battle plan built on the word of God will be the one who will endure to the end. These are the ones who sometimes rise quickly and far up the corporate ladder only to fall down to nothing, enduring the shame and the pain, but like Samson; they build their strength back up one day at a time. This is the power of our belief in Him who is able to give abundantly and exceedingly far above all we are able to ask for. Beloved, the foundation of this battle is Christian belief and values, but the prize is you. Your humiliation and discrediting is Satan's goal and placing the thorny crown of hypocrite on your head is the coronation of Satan's victory.

For we do not wrestle against flesh and blood, but against principalities, against powers, against the rulers of the darkness of this age, against spiritual host of wickedness in the heavenly places (Ephesians 6:12).

Obedience is our first line of defense in this battle for your belief in Christ while living and working in the world and among nonbelievers. We have come through a self-awakening, winding journey of the human mind, heart, and emotions as we have searched for answers from our faith on how we can maintain and sustain a Godly lifestyle while being exposed and attacked by ungodliness on a daily basis. How can we overcome the stain of shame from past mistakes that seem to label and define us? Well, Beloved, as we come to the conclusion of this second book of a three-part trilogy, let me conclude with the principle of obedience.

The prophet and priest Samuel said this:

Has the Lord as great delight in burnt offerings and sacrifices, as in obeying the voice of the Lord? Behold to obey is better than sacrifice and to heed then fat of the rams. For rebellion is as the sin of witchcraft and stubbornness is as iniquity and idolatry, because you have rejected the word of the Lord, He also has rejected you from being king (1 Samuel 15:22–23).

Now as I said, obedience is our first line of defense in this battle. Allow me to point out some Biblical truths and spiritual foundations of the human heart.

Obedience is an essential Christian truth; nothing works without obedience to God's way and word. When I was coming up in the 1960s, 70s, and 80s, I always heard this very famous and yet truthful piece of information. "Boy, a hard head makes a sore behind." Never more true spoken words uttered by the mothers of my generation. The phrase encompassed the fact that if you fail to listen and comprehend and follow instructions, you would feel and be led by these instructions. In other words, if you failed to obey, you will have to sacrifice something.

In the Biblical record, we see that King Saul became king of Israel and Judah by being the people's choice not God's. But God gave the people the desire of their heart for a king like every other sovereign nation around them under one condition which is found in 1 Samuel 12:13–15:

> Now therefore here is the King whom you have chosen and whom you have desired. And take note the Lord has set a King over you. If you fear the Lord and serve Him and obey His voice and do not rebel against the commandments, of the Lord then both you and the King who reigns over you will continue following the Lord your God. However, if you do not obey the voice of the Lord but rebel against the commandments of the Lord then the hand of the Lord will be against you as it was against your fathers.

In other words, what makes this an essential Christian truth is because God desires first a heart that is obedient, pliable, and teachable more so then ritualistic behavior. The sacrificial systems of tithes and offerings and the church system of attendance was never intended to replace living an obedient life, but rather was to be an expression of an obedient life. So what happened with King Saul? Well, we know he was the people's desire and choice to be king, and he led them in the way and word of God. But something began to change in him. The word tells us that he was the people's desire and choice. Beloved, when you become people's desire, you now have some percentage of fame and when your motivation to do what is morally right is dictated by other people's desire for you, you have now become a slave to your fame, position, and title. King Saul found himself in this predicament, and as he became fully motivated by his fame and position, following Gods word and way became a burden to him. He became stubborn and obstinate to the word and way of God, which then turned into outright public rebellion. Then he made an attempt to conceal this rebellion by giving great and expensive sacrifices. I have come to see and know that disobedience always brings sacrifice, and the greater the disobedience the greater the sacrifice. Allow me to give you a very real example of this, in the health care industry, all hospitals and healthcare system providers are inspected by the federal government approximately once every three years, and the bases for these inspections are to see if the hospitals and healthcare system providers are following the guidelines established by the federal government in regards to clinical care, environment of care, pharmacy, medication care, emergency management and life safety systems. When an institution allows these systems to go wanting, through a lack of training, inspecting and concern until they are about to be visited by the federal government, said institution has displayed a disobedient attitude and nature, and because they were not obedient to the guidelines all along, there will be a tremendous sacrifice to bring the institution back into compliance with the guidelines. The sacrifice may involve hundreds of thousands of dollars in overtime spent to fix and clean the place, millions of dollars in purchasing new equipment to replace outdated or broken ones, hiring new and temporary staff, canceling vacations and time off to train and evaluate all staff, and six day workweeks for managers, Everything that was supposed to be done in two years is now being done in a much shorter time period to show and impress the federal inspectors. This type of behavior is not germane to the healthcare industry alone; this lack of concern is the attitude that was the principal reason for the 2008 financial collapse, the saving and loan crisis and the Chrysler automotive collapse in the 1980s, and so on. So my dear friends, as I come to my conclusion of this second installment of this series I pray your strength in the Lord, and until we meet again, always remember the battle is not yours, it's the Lord's. "See then that you walk circumspectly, not as fools but as wise, redeeming the time because the days are evil" (Ephesians 5:15).

END NOTES

- John MacArthur, Author, John MacArthur, editor, *The MacArthur Study Bible* (Word Publishing 1997).
- Owen Williams, *The Corporate Christian: Christian Beliefs Vs. Corporate Behaviors* (Trafford Publishing 2012).
- David Jeremiah, Author, *God in You*, Volumes 1 and 2 (Publishing Walk Thru the Bible Ministries, 1998).
- Jim Rohn, *The Treasury of Quotes* (Sunburst Books, 1996).

MORE ABOUT PASTOR WILLIAMS

Pastor Owen E. Williams is the Pastor of the St. Mark Missionary Baptist church where he has served as senior pastor for the last Seventeen years. He is also the retired Director of Pastoral Care Services at the New York City Health and Hospitals Corporation Kings County Hospital. There, he oversaw the spiritual care for the seven-hundred-bed public hospital. Pastor Williams has a master's degree in Pastoral Counseling, an Honorary Doctorate in Divinity, and a bachelor's degree in Criminal Justice. He is the author of four published books, *The Corporate Christian: Christian Beliefs Vs. Corporate Behaviors, The Corporate Christian 2: The Battle for your Beliefs, The Corporate Christian 3: The Hidden War*, and *American Christianity: Black Liberation White Legalism* the President of the Queens Federation of Churches Board of Directors, former NYPD clergy liaison for the 103rd Precinct, a former member of the Board of Directors for Live on NY, the second largest OPO (Organ Procurement Organization) in North America, and the founder and President of OE Williams Ministries.

Pastor Williams frequently travels to Johannesburg, South Africa, where he conducts training seminars on Solution Focus Pastoral Counseling for social workers, schoolteachers, police officers, and clergy.

Pastor Williams has been married to Elder Debora Williams, his wife for over 32 years, and they have one daughter, Desiree Rose Williams.

Throughout Pastor Williams' Christian journey, the

Lord has taught him many things, but two things have always stayed with him; maximize your moments, we have so few, and an ounce of practice is worth a ton of preaching.

Let us all be practitioners rather than preachers of the gospel, doers rather than hear of the word.

www.ingramcontent.com/pod-product-compliance
Lightning Source LLC
Chambersburg PA
CBHW032056020426
42335CB00011B/369